Praise for *Gentrifier*

"With wry humor and uncommon insight, Anne Elizabeth Moore crafts an intimate portrait of self-determination and communal possibility in a resilient Detroit neighborhood. Yes, this book is about gentrification, but it is also about neighborhood sustainability, government corruption, nonprofit hypocrisy, chronic illness, gardening, girlhood, family, racism, education, misogyny, autonomy, queer striving, a writer's life, and the elusive and ever-present search for home."

—Mattilda Bernstein Sycamore, author of *The Freezer Door*

"Anne Elizabeth Moore is one of our great chroniclers of the collisions between the personal and the political. A contemporary *A Room of One's Own*, *Gentrifier* interrogates the relationships between class, race, gender, religion, sexuality, economics, love, community, and the medical industrial complex, all through the lens of Moore's experience of being given a 'free' house in Detroit. This story of a house, a city, and what it means to be a woman on one's own illuminates the utterly compelling complexities that lie beneath the veneer of what outsiders can glimpse in this one of a kind American city. Moore offers a window through which we can deeply examine the beauties, booby-traps, and at times Kafkaesque logistics of what it means to be an artist in the contemporary Midwestern landscape."

—Gina Frangello, author of *Blow Your House Down*

Praise for *Sweet Little Cunt*
Winner of the Eisner Award

Praise for *Body Horror*
A Chicago Public Library Best Book of 2017
2018 Lambda Literary Award Finalist
2017 Chicago Review of Books Nonfiction Award Nominee

"One of the best Political Economy books of all time."
—*BookAuthority*

"By audaciously linking her disparate *Body Horrors* to a larger construct—more complex even than her own immune system, more menacing than mere patriarchy—Moore allows her essays, each plenty feisty in its own right, to punch significantly above their individual weight. Whether one is ready in real life to attribute everything from Crohn's disease to Pacific Time to the machinations of the market, Moore's arguments land with force enough to make even the marginally politicized reader think."
—*The Los Angeles Review of Books*

"Moore herself is hyper-aware, and her unflinching worldview had the effect on me of a knife cutting through the wool pulled over my eyes . . . Each essay, though varying wildly, held me rapt with its at times heartbreaking, at times serious, at (most) times hilarious excoriation of capitalism and the myriad ways in which it enacts 'heinous acts' upon the marginalized members of our society."
—*Autostraddle*

"Anne Elizabeth Moore's writing is akin to an Olympic gymnast's floor routine. It's strong, precise, sometimes daring and awfully brave about tumbling from one place to another."

—*Detroit Free Press*

"Probing her own experiences with disease and health care, Anne Elizabeth Moore offers scalpel-sharp insight into the ways women's bodies are subject to unspeakable horrors under capitalism."

—*Chicago Tribune*

Praise for *Threadbare*

"Simple, graphic . . . Artfully illuminating." —*Los Angeles Times*

"Useful and engrossing for fashion watchers and women's issues activists, teens, and adults."

—*Library Journal*

"Moore's conversations with sweatshop workers, models, retail clerks, and humanitarian aid workers highlight the vast need for global labor reform—and the arresting visuals are stunning proof of where graphic journalism can go."

—Andi Zeisler, *BitchReads*

"Describing the environmental, social, economic, and personal costs of fast fashion in a style cool as gin, *Threadbare* is both a damning indictment and a stellar example of comics journalism."

—Molly Crabapple

"A quirky, brisk, and piercingly honest recitation of one woman's experience in a post-conflict society overseas."   —*The Rumpus*

Praise for *New Girl Law*

"Post-empirical, proto-fourth-wave-feminist memoir-cum-academic abstract."   —*Bust*

GENTRIFIER

GENTRIFIER

A MEMOIR

ANNE ELIZABETH MOORE

CATAPULT NEW YORK

This book is a memoir. It reflects the author's recollections of experiences over time. Some names and identifying details have been changed to protect the privacy of individuals.

ISBN: 978-1-64622-070-0

Jacket design by Dana Li
Book design by Jordan Koluch

Library of Congress Control Number: 2020952456

Catapult
1140 Broadway, Suite 706
New York, NY 10001

Printed in the United States of America
1 3 5 7 9 10 8 6 4 2

For Thurber, the cat who made me believe in cats,
and for Doly, the neighbor who made me believe in neighbors.

CONTENTS

GENTRIFIER

1

THE HOUSE

A woman must have money and a room of her own if she is to write fiction.

—VIRGINIA WOOLF, *A Room of One's Own*

For the cameras, I pretend that I am seeing it all for the first time. So one evening in early May 2016, families at dinner watch me on WXYZ-TV meandering hesitantly from room to room in the fancy outfit of an award recipient at her own celebratory gala, exclaiming with delight at: Empty white walls! Hardwood floors! A fancy bathtub! My own couch! That Nick and Nadine had carefully packed into a moving van in Chicago the previous day and driven for five hours before installing it in this mostly empty house and then leaving me alone to deal with the organization, the local artists, the new neighbors, the politicians, the print reporters, and the camera crews. The couch, years before, had been a gift from the same two friends, the castaway of a former lingerie designer. My friendship with Nick and Nadine spans more than a decade, and the couch is ten times that old, roughly the same age as the building it now rests in.

My delight at the house, another gift, is unfeigned, even if the structure itself is more familiar than the camera crews portray for viewers at home. For ten years I have spent more time traveling than I have staying put, and I am tired and broke in a general way, although in the moment, I feel happy, relieved, and excited. Those emotions are genuine.

So there's me on TV, smiling and gesticulating exuberantly on the front steps of a cute little white bungalow, shaking the hand of the ward district chief. He presents me with an award. Later he will let my calls about neighborhood needs go unanswered. One of the cofounders of the organization is also there. She hands me a set of keys. Soon she will be the cause of late-night phone calls and several emergency meetings. My next-door neighbors watch eagerly from their own porch. Within a day they will enter my home and explain to me that a neighbor, despite what I may have learned elsewhere, is a best friend. There I am on video, standing between Casey Rocheteau, a poet and educator and the first free-house winner, and the poet Nandi Comer who, it is announced today, will receive the house after mine, making her the fourth free-house winner and the only one from Detroit. Liana Agha-janian, an Iranian American journalist and the second winner, is absent but sends greetings. Collectively, we soon come to share a secret: it can be a nightmare to be publicly awarded a free house.

————

I start my first morning in the house with a cup of coffee on my porch, satisfied with this new life that allows me to be the kind of person who starts a day drinking coffee on a porch. Neighbors emerge, from behind the corners of houses or in windows or walking out onto their own porches. They greet me, cheerily waving or trying a reticent "hello" in English. They are curious about me, and I am also curious about them. The vast majority of them are from Bangladesh. The women wear saris, bright, brilliant draped cloth, or salwar kameez, a long tunic over fitted pants, in yellow with magenta paisleys, or mint green with a floral weave of hot pink and deep purple, or bejeweled turquoise. Head scarves for all the women, equally bright, while the men wear somber, straight-edged caps and beards dyed with henna. It is the American Dream, this drinking-coffee-on-the-porch thing, although it appears to be taking place in Bangladesh.

———

Shortly before I move, I am on a train passing through Michigan in idle conversation with my seatmate. She is older than I am and suffers similar physical ailments, so we swap stories about medications and doctors between comments on the landscape.

"Where do you live?" she asks at one point.

"Chicago," I tell her, "but I will move to Detroit soon."

"Oh, honey," she says, patting my arm. "You're not supposed to say 'Detroit.' Call it southeastern Michigan. Otherwise people will know."

————

The bungalow I move into is built in 1918 and sits on the edge of Detroit, where the city meets its neighbor, Hamtramck. At the time the house is built, the automotive industry is undergoing a boom, not only due to the rising economy but also because its products have become increasingly easy to use. Hand-crank starters—vast improvements over windup spring devices and gunpowder cylinders—begin to be replaced with electric models in Cadillacs in 1912; Ford, the last manufacturer to make the switch, installs the very last of the hand-crank starters in 1919. Electric starters require less upper-body strength to operate and decrease the likelihood that the driver would be run over by their own vehicle while cranking or die in an explosion, so sales— particularly to women—increase; the changeover also necessitates an expansion of the workforce. What eventually becomes my neighborhood is, at the turn of the century, German and Polish, although sometime in the midteens both Dodge and Ford begin recruiting immigrants from elsewhere, too. It is probable, therefore, that the original owner of my house is a European immigrant, lured to the country with a job during the boom at the Dodge Main plant just a mile south, a plant at which parts for Ford vehicles are manufactured.

My father, in the 1970s, collects cars and wants sons; until my brothers are born I am his companion at automotive shows and on Sunday drives in his 1920 Model T. In a flush of enthusiasm for my appreciation of antique cars, my father one day promises me the vehicle when I turn sixteen. Thus it is likely that the original owner of my very first home also has a hand in my very first car.

———

For a full year, every time I am at the house for more than three days in a row, a neighbor woman comes by to inspect my progress unpacking and decorating. Because I spent seven years living on and off in Cambodia, many items I own are immediately recognizable to my neighbors. Without fail, every time a new device or trinket or decoration of South or Southeast Asian origin is unpacked, the neighbor woman's eyes go very, very wide. Her head pulls back and she turns slowly to look at me. Then she points at the object.

"You are Bengali?" she asks.

———

You will remember, perhaps vaguely, that an organization in Detroit started giving away free houses to writers in the mid-2010s—although you may recall instead that it was the city itself giving houses away, or that houses were being given to anyone who asked, or that all housing within the city limits of Detroit had been offered for free to anyone who wanted it, for any reason. Perhaps you heard that the City of Detroit *tried* to give free houses away, but that no one wanted them. None of that is true.

———

I'm in the midst of a health crisis when I first correspond with a new organization in Detroit intending to give free houses to writers. My liver has begun shutting down, although slowly, and it becomes unclear if it will recover, or if I will. During this time I receive a mass email from an acquaintance on the board urging recipients to apply to the program. In my recollection, I read the email and think that the program is a good idea. I click through the application, see that it is extremely short, and resolve to complete it before the deadline. In my recollection, however, I do not complete the application. In fact, as the announcement date of the first winner of a free house in Detroit draws near, and the program is mentioned frequently in conversation or on social media, I berate myself for not having applied.

For this reason, I am surprised one day to receive an email from the organization requesting my social security number and documentation of my recent income. The email is worded confusingly and explains that the information is required to confirm eligibility for the program but states clearly that I am not a finalist for the program.

I send a vague inquiry to my acquaintance on the board wondering why I am being asked for such personal information over email as I am clearly not in consideration for the program, and her response—which fails to acknowledge that I never applied for it—prompts me to search my own email. This is when I discover that I did, in fact, apply to win a free house in Detroit. Keep in mind that I was quite sick. Apparently I filled out the application so quickly that I forgot I had done it at all.

———

When I move into the house my cat is nineteen. Actually I have two cats, but only one has lived with me for nearly twenty years. This is my cat, Thurber. The other cat is All Girl Metal Band. I am not saying she is not worth describing. She is a very good cat. She is soft and sweet and lives up to her name by falling into the toilet or climbing her way onto a high precipice from which she cannot get down without a great deal of hubbub. But she is young and even after seven years I still do not know her as well as I know Thurber. For almost two decades, Thurber and I have traveled the country together, slept together, shared food, communicated wordlessly. So Thurber is my cat. There is also another cat.

The neighbors pick up on this immediately. "How is your cat?" they ask and mean Thurber. Thurber is the one they call chhoṭo bagh, little tiger. Metal Band they call Metal Van, because they can't wrap their minds around an animal named for a joke about a hypergendered musical genre they've never heard of but would hate if they had. I have been unable to properly explain metal bands to them or why I like them. So: Metal Van. They ride one to school every day. OK. But even to them, Thurber is different.

Thurber likes to ride in the car and comment on events we pass by in a language I do not quite comprehend. Thurber believes birds alight on the front porch at my bidding and comes to thank me for them when they appear. Thurber sits at the dinner table when I set a place for him and eats human food off a special plate, unless I feed him with a fork. In this way he grows to like green salad and soup, foods most cats scorn. I celebrate Christmas by making an elaborate meal that Thurber and I eat, together, at the dining room table. I decorate the room to highlight his eye color.

I should admit that the two-year wait between the first mention of my receipt of a free house and the day I move to Detroit offers me ample time to consider the proposition carefully, and I do. But when I take a deep breath, sign the contract, and begin packing, it is because I would like to provide my silly, fuzzy little man a stable place to grow old.

———

Legally, it is not my house. My agreement with the organization stipulates a two-year residence before the title will go in my name. Still, it is called my house in several major newspapers, over the radio many times, on a variety of local newscasts, in international documentaries. The neighbors neither understand nor care about the nuance. To make it easier for everyone, I come to refer to it as my house. Although before I say it out loud, I always hesitate.

———

The word "bungalow" describes a small house with a low-pitched roof, usually only a single story tall, although sometimes one and a half or two. Houses of this design are marked by deep eaves and exposed rafters, an open floor plan, and built-in cabinetry. The term comes from the Hindi word bangla, meaning "belonging to Bengal." The word was first used to describe the detached cottages built for early European settlers in India, hiding its inherent colonialism by paying homage to local culture.

———

In 2013 a new organization based in Detroit announces that it will accept applications from low-income writers for what is described as a free, permanent writer's residency.

The project is one of branding. By the mid-2010s, the media narrative surrounding Detroit has grown far more dire than the city itself will ever be. The image of the once-thriving metropolis now littered with ruins has been affixed to the city for nearly a decade, ever since photographs of formerly thriving factories began circulating online and tour companies set up routes through dilapidated buildings to meet gawkers' demands. In 2009, *Time* runs a cover story, "The Tragedy of Detroit," and any remaining naysayers—often Detroit residents, surviving reasonably comfortably—are shushed. The city is deemed a failure. When Detroit declares bankruptcy and is placed under emergency management in 2013, many feel that something irreversible has taken place. Talk of urban renewal and local boosterism masks horrible mismanagement, the violent seizure of resources, and city residents placed in grave physical danger.

In seeming contrast to the corruption, this new organization is founded. The plan is to install writers in neighborhoods at risk of devastation, places where homes are being abandoned, destroyed, and torn down. That writers really just need a place to get work done—a room of their own—is central to the vision, but the genius of the plan is that it would fundamentally shift the narrative about Detroit by bestowing gifts upon the exact folks who craft narratives for a living. Indeed, the announcement of the project is popular among freelance journalists, who rarely make enough money to accrue a house down payment or earn steady enough income to secure a mortgage. Stories appear from all corners—in several languages—about the genius of a program that gives free houses to writers. It is, indeed, a great idea.

Within months of my arrival in Detroit, however, one of the two cofounders is no longer associated with the project. I hear rumors but never learn precisely what happened. All I know is that one of the people who brought me to the city no longer returns my calls.

———

The house is, let's see: small. There are tiny homes of this same size, although several families of five or six on my block inhabit similarly sized houses quite comfortably. Also I am small, so I do not mind. The front room, which I quickly paint a dark pink the approximate color of liver, has a bay window and is separated from the room behind it by a rounded archway with no ornamentation. This second room, off of which both bedrooms can be found, and which I eventually paint a slate blue, is designated a dining room by design: a hanging light fixture has been hung, low, in the center of the room, necessitating a large table directly under it so that my medium-sized guests do not hit their heads against the glass. The front bedroom has a closet and a window facing the street, and the second bedroom has a panel in the ceiling for attic access, as well as another small closet. Through the dining room is the kitchen, which features one eighteen-inch counter, a sink, a stove, a refrigerator, and a large pantry with a window, from which you can see half the back garden. Off the kitchen is the bathroom, gray, with a shallow, long tub, clean white subway tiles with gray grouting, and a wide sink. There is no shower curtain, but a large plate of thick, immobile glass is secured to the edge of the tub and attached to the wall to contain spray. I am too short for this to be hazardous, although tall friends worry about slicing a jugular if they slip in the shower. The bathroom is gorgeous, the house's only nod to modernism, and featured prominently in photo spreads of the house. The basement—concrete and, standard for the area, prone to flooding—is also accessible through the kitchen, as is the back room, a massive, featureless rectangle with a door to the backyard, one small window, and a concrete floor made softer by bright green, thick, felt flooring. I leave untouched the coat of white primer on the walls in this room only, because it was painted by the organization's board members, a small gesture of my gratitude. In the back are mulberry trees and, eventually, a fruit and vegetable garden, as well as a concrete slab that used to be a garage floor. In the front, two long garden plots for herbs and flowers, a sidewalk that has seen better days, and a long, dirty street connecting, in one direction, to the Davison Freeway and, in the other, to Hamtramck.

The streetlamps on this block are inoperable for years until the organization echoes the community's demands that they be fixed; the city does so, ensuring the one directly in front of my house is particularly bright. This light shines into the window of the front bedroom and, as much as it sends a clear signal to the neighborhood that, at least on one occasion, the city has responded to local needs, I curse it every night.

———

For months, I am booked on television and radio spots. I conduct email and telephone interviews. Two camera crews come by to film two different documentaries, one in French. Also I have a new book out and conduct readings and interviews to promote it. Film options are discussed, agents consulted. It is an exciting time.

I am particularly looking forward to a live video feed for a morning news program in Chicago, where friends might see me as they prepare for work. I have been told that I am to be interviewed about both the house and the book. However, after the hosts greet me cheerily and explain to viewers that I have just won a free house for my writing, they do not ask me anything about what I write. Instead they want to talk about Detroit.

"Aren't all the houses free in Detroit?" the perky blond says.

Her dark-haired male companion belly laughs. "Yeah!" he agrees. "What kind of a prize is that?"

———

My mother is born in the 1940s, so during her lifetime women enter the workforce en masse, earn the legal right to accrue credit in their own names without a male cosigner, are granted the right to be informed of property decisions made by husbands with whom they co-own the property, and win the right to sue for pay discrimination on the basis of gender. The world my mother comes up in as a girl, in other words, only grows to recognize her as a person much later. When I am young and ask her about buying a house, saving money, or investing for retirement, she brushes me off.

"Oh, you don't need to worry about all that," she says. "Your husband will take care of it."

———

After a decade in offices editing magazines, I spend another nine years writing about places where women have explored different ways of navigating economic strife: Tbilisi, Georgia; Leipzig, Germany; León, Nicaragua; Phnom Penh, Cambodia; the Cheyenne River Reservation in South Dakota. If home ownership occurs to me during this time—in the abstract, as I am in no financial position to consider it otherwise—I find the idea vaguely engaging if politically suspect. To live in one place! Forever! Sounds great. But settling in any of the places I come to love would not be an uncomplicated decision. My presence, I see quickly—particularly when paired with Western notions of property ownership—would likely attract further Western, or white, or American, presence. I would, in other words, be acting as a colonizing force, even if I were not technically displacing anyone in the present day and able to look beyond historic colonialist initiatives that I would merely be completing.

So I remain on the move. I become known as someone who will go to unusual locales and write interesting stories, and in this way I build a career. I start saving for a house then—although, again, an abstract one. I resolve to buy a house when it becomes clear where I should live, where I am invited to make a home.

In 2013 I travel two hundred days per year, and the next year starts out no different. Then I become sick and spend the equivalent of a house down payment keeping myself alive. Then I get an email from an organization promising free houses to writers.

———

At one point growing up I am asked if I am rich. I do not think of myself as rich, but I am also aware that I do not think about money very much at all. Neither does anyone I know.

I consider my life from a purely visual perspective. The three-story house I live in sits atop a small hill in St. Paul, Minnesota. Several kids my age live within walking distance, whose fathers are also doctors who collect cars. Large front yard and backyard. Enough food, every day. Neighborhood tucked away, by dint of the circuitous and pretty streets said to have beeen laid out by drunken Irishmen, houses hidden from any real sense of urbanity. A lake place. I have never been to Europe, met a nanny, or had access to more than twenty dollars at a time. I do not think of my family as rich, but I am suddenly aware that the differences between my family and a rich one might not be apparent to other people.

"We're upper-middle class," I respond, a phrase I have heard my parents use.

———

My parents divorce when I am sixteen, and a period of transition follows. My father has been instructed by a judge to financially support the rest of the family, although he does not. My mother, who has not earned wages in many years, and who had chosen to support my father and raise children instead of embark on a career outside the home, must find a job. In a smart move that is not without consequences, she takes a position at my high school, a private college-preparatory institution. This not only guarantees her a wage but also offers her children a discount at the expensive school, which is the only one my brothers and I have ever attended. Somehow this deal comes after the academic year has already started, however, and I've already enrolled in a public high school. It's fine. I excel in my classes and make new friends. When I return to my previous school for my senior year, however, it is clear from the way my family is treated that something has changed, that we are now poor.

———

The process of applying to be awarded a free house includes a video interview during which few questions are posed to me, although I ask several myself. Is any of this real? What are the houses like? Are they inhabitable? How much money will they require to be brought up to code? What is the neighborhood like? Do people bike in Detroit? Have cats? Will I make friends? Find meaningful work? Be happy? The answers are vague but enthusiastic. The houses are great! They just need a coat of paint! Everyone bikes everywhere! Detroit loves cats! There are a ton of places to work! The art scene is incredible! Everyone here is happy!

Of course, I know people in Detroit, and their answers do not correspond precisely to what I am told, but I do not blame the organizational representatives for pride in their own program. The interview goes well. "You are a great candidate," I am told.

A few days before the winner is to be announced, one of the cofounders calls to reiterate. "We want to give you a house," she says. Then the first winner of a free house is announced. It is Casey Rocheteau.

Weeks pass. I receive a call from the cofounder, who acknowledges that the organization awarded its first house to someone else. "We do want to give you a house," she tells me, "but we're going to give you the next one."

This time the process is more elaborate. I visit the house over the winter, meet various people involved in the organization, spend time with friends in town. I ponder seriously whether this house meets my requirements for property ownership and determine that I do indeed appear to be invited to make a home in Detroit. Then this house is awarded to Liana Aghajanian.

I no longer expect a free house. I hope instead to get a good story.

———

By chance I am announced as the next winner of a free house on Equal Pay Day, the spring day U.S. activists mark to call attention to how many more hours women must work than men over the previous year to achieve the same annual rate of pay. Of course, someone complains to the organization on social media that I am the third "female" to receive a free house and suggests men should be given equal chance at the opportunity. (The complainer is incorrect; Casey Rocheteau is nonbinary.) In response, another commenter notes that men might already find current housing options affordable, "given their 30% raise over a woman's pay in most fields." She signs off with a smiley face emoticon.

———

The move begins the period where everyone quotes Virginia Woolf at me. They shake their heads in wonder and say something like, Living the dream, right? *A Room of One's Own?*

I admit that I often scowl. At first I resent the association, because Woolf is a depressive, a modernist, and the only woman writer many who bring her up seem to have heard of. Then I begin to feel as if my situation—white girl in a Bengali Muslim neighborhood in a majority Black city—might appear colonialist enough without bringing an actual Brit into it.

———

There comes a time when it is unclear what I can or should do with my house, when both its legal ownership and its structural

integrity are in question, and I am frustrated with the daily struggles of living in a city with no functional infrastructure. During
this time, a man from across the street tells me in broken English
that he will not allow any new people to live in the neighborhood.
He implores me to continue living in this house forever because,
he says, "this neighborhood is only for us." It is the first time he
speaks to me, although he has waved to me on many occasions.

———————

The day of my arrival I am given a Spirit of Detroit Award, intended to honor significant contributions to the city, although I
have technically made none. Among previous winners is James
Robertson, honored in 2015 for walking close to eight miles between buses each day to his job, as well as thirteen miles back
home each night, ever since his Honda crapped out on him a
decade prior. The so-called Motor City, including the Detroit
metro area—Hamtramck, Highland Park, Dearborn, and various suburbs—was home to competing automobile manufacturing
concerns in the first half of the twentieth century, and the city's
population exploded with workers, who needed cheap, reliable
ways to get to work, and their families, who attended school and
went grocery shopping. Public transportation boomed. When the
car companies left the city for cheaper materials and labor overseas, the infrastructure that supported a bustling public transportation system collapsed. The city that used to make cars was left
then, awkwardly, with only cars as reliable transportation. Besides
walking.

When the *Detroit Free Press* publishes a profile of Robertson in early 2015, it is a story about persistence in the face of crumbling municipal infrastructure. Soon the story changes. Several fundraisers are held, and offers come in from car dealerships. Robertson's story is now about a man of few means receiving a windfall in a cash-strapped town and the forces that seek to take advantage of him. In a follow-up report a year later, Robertson tells reporters that he drives to and from work every day. He says he has lost friends and lovers to tussles over money. He watches more TV than he used to and admits that he has gained weight.

This is the year I accept the Spirit of Detroit Award in my thirteenth hour in the city. The following year, rapper Cardi B is given the same award. It is presented by Kamal Smith, producer for the Hot 107.5 FM show *Morning Heat*. Of the rapper's contribution to the city, Smith tells the *Free Press* on October 30, 2017, "She's definitely big in the Detroit market."

———

Being awarded a house is both validating and terrifying, as well as several other emotions I find myself unable to affix. The plumbing inspector asks me about them one day, these emotions, and I tell him the exact same thing I'm telling you: being awarded a house brings about many diverse feelings. Not the least of them is surprise at the emotional complexity I am willing to display to the plumbing inspector, with little to no prompting.

———

Right around the time of my parents' divorce, my father pulls up the driveway and around the back of the house in his white Jaguar. He has not yet paid any child support, which I know because my mother has repeated this information whenever we complain that meals have become repetitive and sparse.

I am speaking on the phone with a relative, an uncle or aunt. The phone is a large wooden box with separate ear- and mouthpieces, designed after a nineteenth-century wall-mounted telephone. It is positioned directly next to the back door, and slightly too tall for me, so I prop myself up on the balls of my feet to speak into the mouthpiece.

For reasons unknown to me, but not difficult to imagine, my father is no longer allowed to enter our house when my mother is not home, and she is not currently home. What I understand is that he has offered to sell this car, but he has been allowed to keep his black Jaguar. When he opens the back door, jauntily, as if drunk, I pull away from the phone's mouthpiece to challenge him, hoping a question will keep him from entering the house. "You still have that car?" I ask incredulously.

He slaps my face from below with the entire force of his body. This is a surprise; he has previously delivered corporeal punishment only in the context of spankings, although he has more than once used a belt. Thrown off-balance, I hit the phone with my cheekbone and jaw and hear whoever is on the other end of the line ask what just happened, if I am OK. I hang up the phone and go upstairs to my room. I only see him one more time, and then he dies.

———

At some point as a teenager I stop referring to my father as my father, the house I grew up in as my home, or the town I went to grade school and high school in as my hometown. These are terms that should be earned, I explain to friends, and not just applied to whichever persons or objects come closest to fulfilling the roles. I refer instead to my father by his nickname, like everyone else does, like he means nothing to me, my hometown by its proper name, and the house I live in as my parents' house. This is a political decision, one that honors my increasing dedication to using words properly, but technically it leaves me orphaned and homeless.

———

The first few years of my life, I should explain, are spent on the Rosebud Reservation in South Dakota, home of the Sicangu Oyate, also known as the Sicangu Lakota. If you are lucky enough to live there as a white person, you learn quickly how easy it is to grow comfortable on stolen land and how little governments give in compensation for that they take.

———

As I stumble toward adulthood I seek solace in punk clubs, where I drink endless cheap beers out of cans with people who bathe rarely, wear leather, and have relationships with their parents as fraught as my own. This is where I first hear the phrase "property is theft," a translation of French anarchist Pierre-Joseph Proudhon's pronouncement, a vituperative argument against landowners who profit from renting out farmland and housing stock. Most often I hear it when someone grabs a beer that I protest is mine. "Property is theft," some black-clad punk will say as he downs it.

———

The six-year-old who lives across the street is convinced that the reason I cannot enter my attic is that it is where I store the dead bodies. I explain that when the organization decided to renovate the building, they took out the stairs, because they didn't have money to finish the attic. To her it is retribution. She tells me I would definitely still have stairs if I did not keep dead bodies up there.

———

Although I feign surprise at the new house for the cameras, in fact this day has been in the works for two years. Fakery disturbs me, both as a performer and as an audience member. Considering, however, that the keys I am handed unlock the doors of a house that will take another three and a half years to legally come into my possession, that I am told that this house is free when in fact it will cost me close to thirty thousand dollars in repairs and legal fees—six times what the house originally cost the organization—

and that the history of the house, invisible to me at the time, suggests a municipal policy of violence against poor women that my media appearance and the public celebration of my supposedly free house neatly erases, it is unclear to me what degree of complicity I hold in the sham.

———

After the camera crews leave, and the neighbors and organizational representatives go home, I am alone for the first time in weeks. Suddenly in a new city. I have in my pocket a pack of dried pole beans. I am not by any stretch a gardener, just curious, so before I open a single box, I carefully drop the beans into the dirt in my front yard at evenly spaced intervals and, with a paper cup, water them in.

Ten days later, tiny bean plants poke through the dirt. Five months later I make an old family recipe, spicy pickled beans, and send jars to friends around the world.

2

THE NEIGHBORHOOD

We were all being shot backwards and forwards on
this plain foundation to make some pattern.

—VIRGINIA WOOLF, *A Room of One's Own*

At sunset during Ramadan, neighbors bring over quantities of food in Styrofoam containers, enough in each package for three or four people, and boxes from three or four houses, every day. Spicy vegetable fritters, desserts rolled in coconut, rich chicken curries, lamb with rice, naan. It is overwhelmingly kind and unbelievably delicious. I learn which neighbor specializes in which dish, come to associate the smells wafting from windows with gifts that appear later at my door, and begin to discern regional tendencies in food preparation. I receive so many meals that I have trouble eating them all. I learn to stop grocery shopping a few days before Ramadan or I am forced to throw food away.

———

There is a house on my side of the street about six lots south with an overgrown front yard, barely standing chain-link fence, broken front windows, a hole in the roof. Blue paint, formerly vibrant, has peeled from the face of the structure to reveal raw, rotting wood. However, mail is delivered there every day.

According to city bylaws, the building is blighted. The grass, which comes up to my chin, is taller than the allowable four inches; the unrestricted access posed by the broken front windows meets the city's vague definition of a building that is an "attraction to trespassers"; and the hole in the roof grows after each storm, so the structure would appear to present a danger to anyone who enters the facility.

When I ask the neighbor girls about it, the six-year-old across the street chirpily explains that it is the "half-witch house."

"Someone lives there?" I attempt to clarify.

"The half-witch," she says sternly, as if I have not been paying attention.

"But what is a half-witch?" I ask.

"Anne. If she were a full witch, she would fix her roof," the six-year-old says.

———

A lot in my neighborhood holds several parked ice-cream trucks in various states of repair, all year long. Between May and September, three or four of them are likely to be out roaming the area at any time of day, playing attention-getting music on an endless loop. Often the song is the standard, tinny version of "Do

Your Ears Hang Low?" that most recognize as "The Ice-Cream Truck Song," although one or two of the trucks play a particularly grating version of the ditty that inserts someone loudly shouting "Hello!?" between each round. Still other trucks play a random selection of Christmas music. A friend asks the Yemeni family that owns and operates the ice-cream truck empire what compels them to drive around in the middle of summer playing Christmas music day and night on the streets of a mostly Muslim neighborhood. "It is happy music," my friend is told.

———

On my block is a proliferation of landcarpets, usually fancy Oriental rugs laid out on the grass or across the sidewalk, inexplicably there to decorate the out of doors, I imagine, or make for a relatively even dance floor, just in case. On certain plots of land, the carpets overlap and intersect, a mosaic of textiles, my favorite kind of interior decoration. In the Republic of Georgia rugs not only are piled three or four high on the floor but also cover chairs, benches, and tables, and the rich colors and hint of warmth are as intoxicating as the region's wine. Sometimes, rarely, a patterned Oriental in a neighbor's yard will be supplemented by a remnant from some removed wall-to-wall jobber, and it becomes obvious that these rugs serve a purpose, are not only there to visually delight me. Then I see a woman leaning over her landcarpet, lifting up a corner, checking the ground underneath, replacing the landcarpet. Another clue! One day in late fall I eliminate all the weeds from my very narrow side yard in preparation for spring planting.

When I return the next day, my elderly neighbor has laid several ornate carpets on top of my soil. The only English word she ever speaks is my nickname, Annie, and she says it now from her porch while flashing me a thumbs-up.

———

Upon the announcement that I have won a house and am moving to Detroit, a friendly acquaintance asks, gently, what the hell it is that I think I am doing. "I really appreciate your work so I guess I'm just worried about you participating in an org that so blatantly pushes gentrification," she writes me via social media.

It's a fair question. We have few ways of talking about the nuances of the housing crisis in America, so the term "gentrification" often stands in for larger questions about affordable housing, policies of segregation, the displacement of folks of color, nonexistent safety nets for people in poverty, areas with substantial immigrant populations, faulty urban development programs, neighborhood investment, and plain old bad governance. On top of which, let's be clear: white folks moving into communities of color often, if not always, signals trouble.

But the question of my role in the process of gentrification is complex in terms of money. The purchase and renovation of the house, privately funded, do stave off demolition, which would have been publicly funded; in sum, private donors dropped seventy-five thousand dollars total to buy and fix up the house I live in, saving twelve thousand dollars that the city would otherwise have spent tearing it down. This is money that comes from a federal grant called the Hardest Hit Fund, slated to help homeowners at risk of foreclosure. Theoretically, saving the city twelve thousand dollars would help keep families in their homes.

My role as a gentrifier is also complicated by the house itself, which I am told had stood empty for eight years before I move into it. It wasn't selling, the organization assures me. Not to Bengalis, not to white folks, not to anyone at all. If gentrification is the replacement of lower-income residents of a home by middle-class ones, or of folks of color by white folks, or of immigrants by non-immigrants, is it possible if there's no competition for housing?

Indeed, the population decline in Detroit—specifically the effect of the loss of residents in neighborhoods—is largely unexplored in academic or journalistic venues. This, it turns out, is the on-the-ground concern of my neighbors when I move into the area. Neighborhood stability, or whether residents will remain in their houses or move elsewhere—as opposed to economic stability, whether businesses survive in an area—turns out to be surprisingly, achingly real. My neighborhood, shortly before I move into it, loses residents monthly to nearby Warren or the Bengali neighborhood in Brooklyn, New York. The constant loss must be depressing, although the concerns this raises are not emotional but very tangible, my neighbors tell me. If there is no one living next door to you, there is no one to watch your house when you leave, and it will get broken into.

———

The question asked most frequently by my neighbors in my first six months is "Where is your husband?" At first I respond playfully, by looking around frantically and raising my arms up in the air, as if something next to me a moment ago has vanished. I widen my eyes and shrug. I expect that this behavior, repeated, will make my interest in the matter of husbands clear without offering a direct affront to my neighbors' presumptive heteronormativity. However, it is not a question my neighbors are willing to let go, even after husbands consistently fail to appear over the course of several months. Soon the question begins to frustrate me. "Where is your husband?" implies that a husband is required and also that I am in charge of his whereabouts. Often, it is posed while I am carrying a large object or performing difficult manual labor, tasks the questioner implies should be performed by someone else. Moreover, when it is put to me while I am engaged in a strenuous activity, the question is not only judgmental and annoying but also a hazardous distraction.

Once while I am sanding a table in my backyard, the woman next door stops by to say hello. "Where is your husband?" she asks, skeptically looking at the large piece of wood, my gloved hand, the sandpaper. She knows very well that I am not married, as she can see into my kitchen window and through it, even, into my bedroom. She is my next-door neighbor. She watches me hang laundry to dry. She meets every single person that comes to my house. She has even asked me this same question on previous occasions and I have answered straightforwardly that I am not married and explained that I do not want to be married right now, at least not to a man.

"No more husbands," I say to her, sternly.

The way the old-timers tell it, Detroiters used to celebrate Devil's Night—the night before Halloween—by going out en masse to light houses on fire, although things are different now. In 1984 there were 810 fires reported across the city on October 30; in 2018 there are only five. Mischief, small vandalism, and arson have always occurred in the days leading up to Halloween, too, in a tradition that started with far pettier crimes like knocking over trash cans in the 1940s. By 1995, the city had grown frustrated with the constant violence and organized a series of Angel's Night events, including a volunteer patrol. Around fifty thousand people gathered that year to ensure the streets remained free from mischief, often using CB radios, cellular phones, and mounted police-car-like lights to ensure compliance. In 2018, the program is deemed a success. The city cuts funding for the Angel's Night program and begins, once again, to host Halloween parties for kids. Local reporters, however, track an uptick in arson in the days before the Fourth of July.

When my neighbors decide to paint their houses, it is usually with leftover paint from another project: turquoise, from a bedroom remodel; pink, made from a forgotten can of white and the maroon of the entryway. No one ever consults a neighborhood association or complains that a house is too garish, and the houses never are.

One day, you just come home to find the porch of the house four lots south of yours has gone a dark bluish green or the faces of the bricks have been painted a primary red and the mortar carefully redone in white, like a child's depiction of a house made manifest. A bit farther away, one of my neighbors has constructed a full sauna in his garage; another has purchased several disused houses in the neighborhood and turned each into a different kind of artistic space: Sound House for noise experimentation, Squash House for community gatherings at the brightly colored abode. Play House is what the name implies: a theater, eminently reconfigurable around each performance. A block and a half away is a neighbor-created skate park. It is basically true that the large-scale creative projects in the neighborhood are implemented by white artists and individual home improvements are offered up by Bengali and Yemeni residents, but the continuum of whimsical reuse in the area feels all of a piece.

————

The organization sends someone over to visit—a tourist, in town checking out sites of interest—and because no further explanation for his presence is offered, I assume he is a potential funder. He is certainly rich, a white dude who name-drops famous but boring people and is wearing, inexplicably, a suit coat, matching pants, and a vest on an extremely hot summer day. He even passes the millionaire test: a pair of pants I own that everyone hates except millionaires. I wear them at fancy summer parties, on boats or for new buildings, and I always receive compliments from the boat's owner or the man whose last name appears on the new facility. "I love your pants," the suit-wearing man now says. He asks how I like the neighborhood, specifically wondering if I feel isolated.

"Sometimes I do," I say. A moment of honesty. We are standing in my front yard.

He nods knowingly and gestures at my neighbors' houses. "Yes," he says, "these people are not the smartest." He grits his teeth and grimaces in support of his own statement.

I panic. It is a mistake to assume that my neighbors don't understand English, even if they do not wish to speak it to him. I look around and hope they have not heard, and if they do, that they do not believe I agree with him. Then I panic again because I feel I must respond to him as if it were a totally acceptable thing to say, in case he wants to give the organization money.

———

The older neighbor girls—Nishat, next door, and Sadia, across the street from Nishat—sit on their front porches in the summer evenings and loudly discuss the activities of YouTube celebrities. When they have something more private to address, they quickly announce that they are going for a walk and they parade down the long block on my side of the street, cross the street to the corner store that will soon burn down, peruse the goods for a moment, and then make the return trip on the other side of the street toward Sadia's house at the end of the block. For weeks, I am jealous of their clique, for they are the cool kids, even though no one seems to recognize it yet. Then one night they invite me to go to the store with them. I dub the nightly walk their Evening Constitutional and soon join their ritual. We talk about normal things: School, boys, unusual houses, the people we meet. The city. For one whole summer, however—the summer Sadia is fourteen and two of her sisters have babies—Sadia does not come outside at all. She is working, caring for newborns, and no longer has time.

Her brothers' schedules remain undisturbed.

———

The six-year-old across the street yells my name when she wants to talk to me. She is too young to cross the street by herself, so sometimes she comes out onto the porch first or descends the first couple of stairs to the sidewalk. The questions she asks are ponderous. She will ask, "Anne, did you know?" and then she will ask about something I could not possibly have known, such as something she did earlier that day or something she invented or dreamed. She often asks questions about my cats, such as what they are doing right at that moment, which is the kind of thing she could answer herself if she were able to cross the street. She does not wait until I am visible on my porch to ask me questions, or in my front garden, nor does she always come outside to ask them. I occasionally hear her, yelling my name from inside her house, when I am sitting in my living room, or in my bedroom.

———

I am driving on the Davison Freeway heading toward the 10 about two and a half blocks east of my house when a car veers off in front of me and screeches to a halt at the side of the road. I slow, in case assistance is required, and as I approach the vehicle, the man in the driver's seat throws open his door and leaps out of the car. Then he runs around the other side of the hatchback, swings open the passenger-side door, and throws a punch at the person still seated. Other vehicles begin to pull over, keeping some distance, as the man yanks a woman out of the car to a standing position by the collar of her T-shirt, then punches her again. She breaks into a run, across traffic, which would be dangerous if all the cars had not already slowed or stopped on the freeway. "I'm calling the police!" one guy in a stopped car screams out of his window, as the driver sprints after his prey. The news doesn't seem to affect him. Eventually sirens approach.

The six-year-old across the street, always jealous of my cats, begins telling me about her own kittens. She claims they live in her garage but that we cannot see them. It is unclear if they are real. Does she mean that they are invisible kittens or that she will not allow us to visit them? This is also unclear. Her little sister, five, who speaks only enthusiastic gibberish, does not help.

Soon the questions about kittens become very specific, and it grows clear that her kittens are indeed real. But still she will not allow us to see them. She cannot answer questions about the kittens' origins or age, because she does not know how babies are born and does not grasp the concept of time. Still, everyone is very excited.

Then a tragedy occurs while I am traveling, and when I return no one mentions the kittens again.

———

That first summer, a neighbor's pumpkin falls into my yard and decomposes in the soil and I do not notice. My second summer, pumpkin plants grow from every crevice, vining up every fence, stick, gate, and other plant that they can find. I let many of them fruit and grow fifty-two Baromasi pumpkins that year, a light, delicious breed of squash that is more watery and tastes sweeter than the pumpkins I am used to. They are excellent for making soups and breads, but I find that after I have eaten my way through two pumpkins I no longer have the will to consume any more. I give several away as gifts and load the neighbors up with as many as they can carry, but still I am left with thirty spare pumpkins the week before Halloween. None of the neighbor kids have ever carved pumpkins, partially because their families are from Bangladesh and partially because the holiday has been largely criminalized in Detroit for over two decades. By luck, Nick and Nadine come to town and together we gather up sharp knives and spoons, spread a tarp across the front porch, and invite all the young neighbors over to spend a day carving the extraneous gourds into hideous faces. As it grows dark I light candles and drop them inside the pumpkins. We line them all up on my front steps so the whole neighborhood can see the young people's hard work from their own houses. The children are delighted. Finally, Halloween! Their mothers are angry at me for wasting food.

———

Occasionally, the men in the neighborhood wander into my backyard to watch me work. At first I am unnerved, because I cannot understand what they say to each other as they point to and discuss my activities. I am also certain they will later consult with their wives, who will then come by to inquire after the whereabouts of my husband. Sometimes, however, one will utter, "Good idea," in response to something I am doing, or nod in approval. The men have at times heated discussions, near arguments, about my process, although in Bangla, and no translations are made available. They offer no help. On one particularly frustrating day, when their discussions about my work grow quite loud, I challenge the committee. I'm hoping they will retire to a front porch or take a walk through the neighborhood for amusement instead of watching me work. "Can I get you anything?" I ask, impolitely.

"Oh, no," my next-door neighbor explains, Nishat's father. "We have just never seen a white woman work so hard."

They stay where they are and continue their discussion.

———

I order a large plastic tank to build a water irrigation system and it is delivered in a massive cardboard box, which I leave on the front porch.

"What's the box for?" Sadia asks.

"I bought a human-meat grinder," I tell her. "I can fit a whole kid in there, make some hamburger."

"Oh," she says, unimpressed, already used to me. "Can we use it as a time machine?"

"Sure," I say.

———

My first Thanksgiving in Detroit, I make a traditional turkey dinner and share it with my neighbors. For this I must acquire a halal turkey, and when I order it I am surprised to be asked if I would like it alive or dead. "Dead," I say cautiously, now unsure what I have gotten myself into. The proprietor of the spice store that somehow also acquires halal turkeys nods appreciatively and writes my name down incorrectly. When I pick up the turkey, it still has feathers, as well as a neck, so I frantically consult the internet for advice. Luckily I already own an ax, for eradicating the many stumps from the backyard, and harbor the patience to pluck out feathers. I eventually cook the turkey, and make gravy, and craft a cornbread stuffing as well as cranberry sauce and green beans. I spend the day carving the turkey, which I also learn how to do from internet videos, and divide it and the sides into six Styrofoam cartons, which I then deliver to all the houses on the block that feed me every Eid plus the sole Black family in the neighborhood, a few houses away. I deliver the meals, thrilled by the experience and delighted to be paying my neighbors back for their kindness. Everyone thanks me politely except the Black neighbor boy, who opens the container and begins eating its contents immediately, turning away from me without shutting the door. I notice that he is alone in the house. He and his family move away a few months later.

———

The house to the north of mine has an empty lot next to it, as does the house to the south. There is an empty lot next to the house across the street, as well, and another three houses away. That is just on this half block. There is an empty lot about seven houses south, too, and two more before the block ends on this side of the street, another two on the other side.

Instead of thinking of them as blank spaces, or ruins, I come to learn the story of each particular vacancy, what precisely was lost, and when, and who suffered. When the family left, what they were like, what came after, how long the house stayed, how it deteriorated. It becomes possible to read the history of each particular empty lot by the scars it has left on the soil or nearby houses or neighbors.

The empty lot next to my neighbors to the north, I am told, was a house until the New Year's Eve before I moved in, when the house caught fire. It burned so hot the fire leapt to my neighbors' house, too, and melted the siding on the house on the other side. That family, a few houses north of me, never repairs the siding and it remains, bubbled and charred, hanging ineffectively off the side of the house for years.

The burned house itself remains standing, blackened and unsteady, for months. It is the public celebration of my move that convinces the city to clear the burned shell away. When the lot comes up for sale, the city sells it to my neighbor for one hundred dollars. He says he will build a playground for the kids, but he just parks cars on it.

————

The six-year-old across the street is visibly confused when I mention America. "I've heard of that place," she says.

I assume we are playing a game where we imagine we live somewhere else. "You have! Do you like it there?" I ask.

"I don't know," she says, as if I am somehow putting her on.

"Well, we are there right now. We are in Detroit, which is a city in America," I explain.

"What?" she says. She is both annoyed and confused. I repeat myself. She eyes me evenly and takes a moment to compose her thoughts.

"When I was born, I lived in Bangladesh," she says to me. At first it looks as if she will continue, but she does not. Our discussion ends there. It is unclear whether this refutes my theory about living in Detroit or not. I decide that I do not care, either way.

————

One very hot Eid, I come across a handful of men in the yard of the half-witch's house. Many of them are men that have come to my own backyard and amused themselves by watching me work.

I am interested to see that, here, the men are actively engaging in very strenuous work, particularly on the holy day. A man in a glistening white outfit and matching cap, who is nonetheless using a machete to trim the front foliage, waves. "Hello, neighbor!" he says.

"Eid Mubarak!" I reply. "What are you doing?"

"Our neighbor," he says, "she will lose her house if we do not help her. So we help her."

The men toil until nightfall. The woman who lives in the house never emerges.

———

The first time I load up my truck bed full of cow manure from the community garden, I ask my neighbors if they want any poop, and I am treated with disdain, as if I am a disgusting person. After the Year of the Many Baromasi Pumpkins, however, everyone wants some poop.

"Anne, when will there be poop?" one older woman asks me, very seriously, adjusting her head scarf.

———

It is true that if I ask my neighbors for news, they are as likely to mention a crime a few blocks away that occurred the night before as they are an election or natural disaster in Bangladesh.

———

My internet goes out. A service tech comes to investigate. He tells me he used to live in the neighborhood, two blocks north, and that all the cable lines in the area are in horrible disrepair. We talk for a long time. I ask why he left the neighborhood.

"My girl, she was havin' a baby," he says, "and the day we found out, we got our car broken into and then someone lit our house on fire. I was like, 'That's it.'"

He moved twelve miles away but says he didn't want to go too much farther than that because he likes his job with the internet service company. "Thing is, though," he tells me, "service never worked in this neighborhood. It's a low-priority area. They just don't wanna fix it. Too many poor people, too many immigrants." At home, he says, he uses a competing internet company.

———

On a walk through the neighborhood one day, I ask one of the young women I meet about her father. He is an extremely imposing man, nearly terrifying in appearance and demeanor. I gather he is a religious leader of some kind but know he does not currently teach Arabic or the Koran, nor does he appear to lead a mosque. I have recently learned, however, that he used to teach Arabic, so I ask my neighbor if her father would like to teach Arabic again.

"Oh, he is too busy," she says.

I ask what he is busy doing, and she gestures vaguely. "But what does he do for a job?" I ask directly.

"He is," she starts, gestures again, and then says, "an exorcist.

But we don't like to talk about it with outsiders, because they will not understand."

I ask no follow-up questions.

———

I place a hammock on my front porch so I can lie in it and read and write during the day. I like to think I am performing for my neighbors the life of a writer, expanding their idea of women's labor, but when they come over to say hello, they tell me that they, too, like to "play Facebook." They do not respect writing as labor and send their children over to talk to me or play near me while I am working. Sometimes they leave their young children near me and then go somewhere else, or inside, expecting that, because I am not doing anything and a woman, I am, of course, watching their toddlers. I come to learn that when they ask if I am working today—which they often do while I am in the process of working—they mean: Will you be doing manual labor?

———

One day, as I am passing by the house the children call the half-witch house, a blond, white woman comes out of the front door. I am so stunned to realize that there is another white person on my block that I fail to recognize that she is the person I have come to think of as the half-witch. I wave and smile, and she nods on her way to the mailbox but does not engage me in conversation before returning to her house.

"You guys! I saw the half-witch!" I tell the neighbor girls.

"What's a half-witch?" the six-year-old across the street asks. "That doesn't make any sense. You can only be a witch or not."

———

Bengali people start settling in this area sometime in the 1980s, although my neighbor, who arrives as a young man, recalls that the neighborhood at the time is still mixed and underpopulated. A mass exodus from Queens at the turn of the century brings another eight thousand or so Bengalis, *The New York Times* reports in a March 8, 2001, article. The *Times* attributes the move to rock-bottom rents and the rumor of jobs at a handful of new Bengali restaurants opening nearby at the time, although certainly the vibrant Muslim population of nearby Dearborn helps establish a larger sense of community. In truth, however, no one can really explain why this area became a destination for Bengali immigrants, although I can see clearly that proximity to family and space to garden are both prized. The population change over the decades is significant: from a few thousand Bengalis in the 1990s to approximately twenty thousand Bengalis today. The city capitalizes on the renown in 2017 and, in a public ceremony, officially deems the neighborhood Banglatown.

———

Strays begin gathering in my yard. In the winter, a wide white cat with black markings and several facial scars makes his home on my front porch. I catch him eating from my garden, his jaws locked on a forgotten pumpkin, and name him Culprit. I begin feeding him, and it turns out he is kind and intelligent. Thurber is interested, attentive, but does not want to engage with this cat. Metal Band feels betrayed by every bowl of food I give him. Culprit, meanwhile, would very much like to come inside and live with us.

———

One day I come home from an errand and, while fetching some grocery bags out of my truck, realize the women gathered on the porch across the street are talking about me in jealous tones. "You are lucky to drive," one comes over to say to me, solemnly. Most of them aren't allowed to, she explains, or they secretly know how to drive but don't have permission to use family cars. A few more women join us. One points to another and explains that she knows how to drive but has never been taught how to park. I see for the first time that they occasionally think me lucky to have no husband and no kids, even if they also believe I must be lonely because I am the only person that lives in my house.

———

The bank teller requests identification when I open an account. "Do you even like it here?" she asks, examining my Illinois driver's license. "After Chicago, isn't it sort of like living on the farm?"

She means this as a metaphor, as if I have moved from the big city out to some quiet rural habitat with only a cow for a friend. She doesn't know I have just been at the garden center, where I re-upped my strawberry starters, picked up some manure, and grabbed a new packet of spinach seeds. She doesn't know that the night before, I'd eaten my first meal comprising mostly greens I had grown myself, topped with a salad dressing I'd concocted from herbs and homemade vinegar. She doesn't know that before I unpacked, I dropped several beans in the ground in my front yard, hoping an elaborate growth of fruit-bearing vines would curl up my porch, or that my neighbor side-eyed me then and asked why I didn't want pretty flowers in front of my new, pretty house. Later, this same neighbor found some lima beans from her country abandoned in my backyard and shelled them into my hand, conveying through gesture what I was to do with them. I planted some in my front yard, too, and now that the lima beans are coming in alongside the Kentucky ones, she couldn't be more excited. "If your beans come in first, I will borrow them," she says. Even the across-the-street neighbor, a man of some stature, has come by to express his enthusiasm for the front-yard bean-growing project.

"It is a little bit like living on a farm," I tell the bank teller. "That's what I like about it."

———

Local ice-cream trucks are governed by an alternative set of rules to those by which most vehicles abide. They can, for example, drive the wrong way down a one-way street and park wherever they like. They may park next to you, on the street, and you will be unable to move your minivan. You might be able to say to the driver, "Will you move your truck? I must go to the hospital for an emergency," but the driver is as likely to say OK as he is to not move his truck. The ice-cream truck may target a family, usually a family with children. Often the children run outside immediately and order and receive their ice cream, and then the truck will pull away to the next house where children reside. Sometimes the children do not come outside, however, due to illness or punishment or absence. Then the ice-cream truck will either drive away after some time, or not. It may park there, playing its song, for a very long time, as if punishing the neighborhood for housing insufficiently excitable youth. When I first move to the neighborhood, and it is not yet locally known that I do not eat dairy or sugar, the ice-cream truck parks directly in front of my house for an hour or so, sometimes longer, at least three separate times.

———

There is a knock on my door one afternoon while I am working. When I open the door, it is a man who lives several houses south. He is generally unfriendly and ignores me when I say hello, sometimes also turning away aggressively, or muttering something to his children, who are also unusual in that they do not speak to me. He is a tall and thin man and employs overly formal mannerisms, like an undertaker. He asks to borrow a glass of water.

I am confused. Has his water been shut off? Is there not a house nearer to his that has running water? Why would he come to me, someone he appears to hate? But he does not answer questions regarding his need for the water. Nor does he have a cup to place the water in. Does he want filtered water or tap? He only repeats himself: "Please, a cup of water."

I ask him if someone is going to drink it. If so, I do not want to give him tap water, which has recently been shown to carry Legionnaires' disease, hepatitis, and lead particles.

"My wife sick" is how he responds.

I look outside, over his shoulder. The wife is there, pale but livid, staring at me. Her hair is unwashed, oily and wavy down the sides of her gaunt face. The other houses are eerily abandoned for the middle of the day and I am becoming quite nervous. Also the man refuses to enter my house. It is as if the idea disgusts him.

I fetch him a cup of filtered water in a plastic cup and an Emergen-C packet. "This will be good, too, if she is sick," I tell him, holding out both and gesturing toward her.

"No!" he says, taking only the water from my hand and backing away from the door. "For hair. Water from seven families will wash her hair. Then, better."

———

Three and a half years after I move to town, the City of Detroit designates two sidewalk slabs in front of my neighbor's house as worthy of replacement. These particular slabs are exactly as bad as the slabs next to them, exactly as bad as every other slab of torn-up concrete along the walkway in front of all the houses on this block. The slabs in front of my house, for example, have been eroded entirely, just rough pebbles now, stuck in concrete, difficult to shovel in winter or traverse in bare feet in summer. A two-man crew removes the old slabs, pours in new concrete, and then leaves to replace two other concrete slabs in the sidewalk across the street, seemingly chosen at random. The neighbors follow the pair as they go about their duties and eventually ask the workmen why they are replacing these slabs, but not the ones next to them, just as bad.

"These are the ones we were told to replace," the workmen shrug.

———

The girls and I take an Evening Constitutional one hot night to gossip about our neighbors. Who is moving away, who is cute, who is having babies. Sadia spots a handwritten sign in Bangla tacked to a front porch and points to it, eyes wide, meeting Nishat's gaze.

"What is it?" I ask. "Are they renting their house?"

"It is an advertisement," Sadia explains in hushed tones when we have passed out of earshot of the residents of the house.

"For a wife!" Nishat exclaims loudly.

———

After a year of living in Banglatown, I go to fill up my car's tank at my favorite local gas station in a brightly colored, paisley-patterned dress. It is a sunny, happy day, and the proprietor greets me cheerfully when I enter the station to pay for my gas. "Today," he says

grandly, widening his arms, "you look like a Pakistani woman."
He is from Pakistan. "But don't worry!" he adds when I give him
a look of dismay. "I know you are really from Bangladesh."

———

I invite several friends to live in my house for two weeks and make
comics and zines with me and my neighbors, and although it is
Ramadan and everyone is fasting, Nishat comes and joins us almost every day. The younger girls, and Sadia, come occasionally.
It is my first summer in Detroit—in fact, I have only been in
residence for two months—and I am unsure what to expect from
their participation. However, I have traveled around the world for
several years making zines with young women and expect that
the practice will become a regular part of our future together.
The neighbor girls are diligent and engaged and thrive on the
attention of the diverse group of women. They learn the basics of
comics and zine-making. When the two-week period is over, my
friends go back home. The neighbor girls hand me a gift: a col-
laboratively written, hand-drawn and colored book describing my
two-month history in the house. It becomes my most cherished
possession in Detroit, made more valuable by the fact that I can
never again convince Nishat and Sadia to make zines with me.

———

Usually when I pull out my push mower, Nishat's mom berates me
for using it. Her husband elaborates. "I have one of these," he says.

"You work, all day, then have a heart attack. Still there is more lawn." They demand that I cease mowing and let them take care of the task with their gas-powered mower. It is a fight I rarely win.

Yet one day as I mow, Nishat's mom comes to explain that it has been raining every day, and the grass keeps growing, but something has gone wrong with her mower. She asks to borrow mine.

"Oh, no," I say, for this is my chance to return the favor. "I will do it." She protests mildly until I point out that her outfit would become covered in grass and dirt and that she would sweat, so she sits on the stoop and chats easily with me while I mow her lawn with my push mower. A woman across the street comes over, with snacks, and the conversation switches to Bangla. The two neighbors sit chatting happily, pointing out inconsistencies in my mowing technique and offering me slices of apple.

———

The neighbor girls and I take an Evening Constitutional in late spring and discover that the front door of the half-witch's house has come off a hinge and is hanging ajar in the frame.

"Uh-oh," I say, pointing to the door. "Is she OK?"

Nishat becomes excited. "I forgot to tell you! I saw her at my school one day! She was walking by during recess and went next door to the church where they serve meals." She wanted to talk to her, she explains, but felt like it would be a violation of her privacy.

Six months later we are on another walk. It is late fall and growing cold. This time, the roof of the house has fallen through. The door is missing. The grass has become overgrown again. A wheat-pasted notice on the front of the building says the house has been slated for demolition.

3

THE DATE

This is an important book, the critic assumes, because it deals with war. This is an insignificant book because it deals with the feelings of women in a drawing-room. A scene in a battlefield is more important than a scene in a shop—everywhere and much more subtly the difference of value persists.

—VIRGINIA WOOLF, *A Room of One's Own*

Lord, if I had a quarter for every dude who wrote to "welcome" me to Detroit by offering me "a tour of the D."

———

I name the house Catroit, Michigan, and plan elaborate cat ramps to run through each room for Thurber and All Girl Metal Band. I have a silver plastic nameplate made up and paint the front door a bright red, right away. Then I install the nameplate on the newly red front door, directly under the peephole. I photograph this and replace all my online avatars with this image of permanence, a statement that indicates I am a good provider for my animal friends. I think it hilarious, a ridiculous take on stately writers' mansions that I still seek to emulate. Edith Wharton's house in the Berkshires, the Mount, which she called her "first real home." Eugene O'Neill's family residence, Monte Cristo Cottage, in Connecticut. Pearl S. Buck's Green Hills Farm in Pennsylvania. Beatrix Potter's Hill Top. Catroit, Michigan. The name is self-aware, marginally pretentious, and ultimately a joke about cats and placemaking. Everyone who knows me says, Oh, haha, of course, that is so you.

A new, local Facebook friend sees my updated avatar and attributes the nameplate to one of the men associated with the organization. He congratulates me for being the recipient of such a good, funny joke that, clearly, a man made. Then he asks if I would like to have coffee. I tell him that I would not.

———

After it is announced that I have won a house but shortly before I move into it, I meet with a male journalist for drinks. He asks me about the house and expresses jealousy at the stability it will allow for in the extremely tumultuous field in which we both work. Then he segues into more questionable conversational territory, wondering aloud why I deserve a house, in comparison to someone like him. He lists his accomplishments. He concludes these musings by requesting, perhaps jokingly, that I let him live in my house with me. "I don't cook," he says, as if having to also prepare meals for him might seal the deal.

———

When I was little, and for a long time after that, my gender was "girl-ish" and my sexuality was "But maybe I don't want to date men?" This is about twenty-nine steps removed from lesbianism, in case you're keeping track, but by the time I move to Detroit I have not dated a man in several years.

———

Standing on his porch as if it were the bow of a ship, my neighbor spots a disturbance in the water. It is the bright blue recycling bin I am hauling to the curb. The city's recycling program is in its very early stages, although there are rumors that separating recycling from garbage will soon become mandatory. It never happens. More often than not, the city fails to pick up my recycling at all. "Oh," he says loftily, "for fancy garbage."

"Or, like, glass and cardboard?" The bin is currently filled with my moving boxes.

"Yes," he says in full agreement, "I suppose if you drink that much every week, it will be important."

"Yes," I say, "I will do my best." Soon I will learn that he is a now-devout Muslim who spent a decade clubbing in New York and loves to swap drunken-night-out tales, but at this moment I only know that he sometimes comes over to watch me perform manual labor.

He catches me by the arm then, lightly, to underscore that he is joking. "It's OK," he says reassuringly. "We are very open here. We love everybody. You can drink as much as you want, and whoever sleeps over—girls, boys—we don't care! We are open!"

———

I flirt easily with a man at an event I am covering as a reporter who turns out to be a good source for a story I am writing about the housing crisis. Unfortunately it is too late to initiate a relationship on purely professional terrain, and he interprets every request for information I make as more flirtation. In fact, he withholds information from me, flirtatiously, unless I agree to a date with him in the future. When I call him one day with a minor query after some documents he has promised, he suggests I call him back later that evening at his home number and the conversation moves quickly to less professional matters. I explain that I cannot go out with him until after my deadline and hope this will be read as a strict boundary, but I know already that I will tolerate his behavior because he is the first person I meet outside of the organization that gave me the house who appears to read books.

———

I own a pair of dark purple, patent-leather, off-brand Doc Martens–style boots that I purchased on sale because they hold a pair of orthopedic inserts and look OK—just OK—but these boots are otherwise unremarkable. They are the kind of clothing I might have worn as a kid when I played dress-up, a young person's idea of adult footwear, but now that I am an interesting adult I find my tastes are so much more elaborate than I even understood was possible at the time: silver knee-high boots, green suede ankle boots, snakeskin strappy heels. In fact, these are just regular dark-colored shoes and, because they hold my orthotics, are quite comfortable. I wear them almost every day. I have worn them in Chicago and New York and Toronto and on book-tour stops around the country. Everywhere they go unnoticed. Except in Detroit. Every time I wear them, someone says to me, "I love your shoes!"

————

For several weeks, the man I flirted with at an event who turned out to be a good source for a story will only respond to me via dating app, so I am forced to log in to Tinder every time I need information about the housing crisis.

In this way I find myself dating again.

————

The self-checkout line at the grocery store is the correct line to stand in if one wishes to avoid conversation, but the man in front of me wants to talk about what I am buying, how I will pay for it, and how it is not very much food so will I come back again tomorrow? He is significantly older than I am, and his method of inquiry is paternalistic, meaning that he does not ask me questions to hear my answers but asks so that he can tell me what I should do instead of whatever it was I just said. I respond, happily, because this is not a taxing interaction for me, once I catch on to the game. In fact, it is almost as good as having no conversation at all. He just wants to talk. He does not particularly care what I say.

Until he asks if I am married. This question seems to come out of nowhere, since we have just been talking about salad and how it is easier to use a credit card at a checkout machine than cash. My muscles tense. "No," I say, because I am not married. I ask why he wants to know.

"So I can take you out on a date," he says. "Somebody already own you, I don't wanna go there."

"Oh," I say. "No thank you."

———

I meet a woman during a book event in Canada and we converse easily. She is funny and sharp and beautiful in an undiscovered-Hollywood-starlet way. Soon we are texting, then texting many times per day, mostly jokes about things we see as we go about our days in separate cities. Because she is conversant in harm-reduction techniques and international sex work legislation, the latter the topic of my recent book, I deduce that she is a sex worker. We discuss it and thereafter talk about both her work and mine openly.

What this changes in our relationship is very slight but notable. She is no longer concerned about what I might say about her job, so speaks more easily about her day, but is increasingly concerned that our conversation will be recorded by unknown parties. Perhaps only sex workers and journalists are aware that this is no mere paranoia. In fact, I use a secure messaging app precisely to allay this fear and suggest she download it as well. However, installing it on her phone does little to quell her concerns. If she is flagged as a sex worker and tries to cross the border into the United States, she may be turned away, she reminds me. This has happened to people we both know. Her concern deepens as we first joke about, and then discuss more seriously, a visit to Detroit.

She begs me to delete every text message after every conversation, but as a writer in the early stages of a long-distance relationship, I find that I cannot. It would leave me with no evidence, no anchor, no sense of the other person, I contend. We agree to a compromise, wherein I set all messages to disappear after a week. I am confident that this has resolved all issues, since the only way to access our correspondence would be to download it directly from my phone within six days. Under what circumstance would that ever happen?

One night we stay up late texting about her mother, who comes to visit, and her mother's intolerance of her occupation. The next night, I attend a film festival on assignment. The opening is in Windsor, Ontario, a twenty-minute drive away, and the trip there is uneventful. On the return, however, border security on the American side aggressively questions me about my travels, my work as a journalist, whom I was visiting in Canada, and why I was there. After several rounds of gruff queries and a visual survey of my empty pickup truck, two officers demand I get out of my vehicle, leave the keys in the ignition, and place my cell phone unlocked on the dash. As I wait inside for the half hour it takes for officers to go through my scant belongings, it gradually dawns on me that border patrol officers now have access to the extremely intimate late-night concerns of a Canadian sex worker.

Two years later, the warrantless search and seizure of cell

phones, a practice that appears to have targeted journalists cross-
ing into Mexico and Canada from the United States, will be declared unconstitutional. But by then our correspondence is long
over.

———

My deadline looms and the source for my story is the man with
whom I accidentally flirted and with whom I communicate primarily via dating app. He has not yet sent the information promised. When I call him to put in another request, he becomes
incensed and accuses me of harboring "the wrong idea." He hangs
up on me, angrily, and I never receive the documents. I am also
confused.

———

When the house is first sold to the organization, mulberry bushes,
famously pernicious, have taken over the backyard. Many have
grown into small trees, four to six inches thick, with thin roots
spreading quickly to every available patch of soil. A team of vol-
unteers comes before the house is given to me, and the trees and
bushes are cut to stumps, eight to ten inches out of the ground, to
facilitate removal. Mulberry bushes grow quickly, however, and
most exhibit new growth within days.

It takes a full year to eradicate these stumps from my backyard. Except for when I am writing or taking care of other basic needs, I spend every waking moment of that year poisoning,

burning, cutting, and digging out the plant. The work is difficult, because the roots are skinny and long, and there seems to be an infinite number of them. To get to the roots, I find I must cut away all of the quick-growing, leafy branches of the plant first, although the plant continues to grow even as I hack at it violently. I do not own expensive tools, only a shovel, some matches, salt, a small ax, and various pairs of pruning shears, so most of my efforts are less effective than they would be if I purchased the proper tools for the job. I refuse to buy them, however, because doing so would be a financial investment in something that I wish did not exist.

In contrast, performing the work feels enjoyable, meditative. As I do it I think at first that I might compose an essay on digging out stumps and ponder the language I could use to describe my methods, but it soon becomes clear that most of the metaphors available to describe similarly frustrating endeavors are literal descriptions of removing stumps—digging deep, growing like a weed, pulling something out by the root, feeling stumped.

Because the practice I am engaged in daily is so widely understood to be filled with frustration that descriptions of it act as metaphors for other, less taxing undertakings, I do not write about it. I even stop talking about it.

———

Between part-time teaching, writing, and living in a community in which I speak none of the primary languages, my sense of isolation quickly becomes extreme. My refusal to speak on certain subjects that affect me daily is alarming, dysteleological for a writer. I determine to seek professional help and visit a therapist. During my visit, she has me fill out an elaborate intake form, including check boxes for gender, race, language spoken in the home, sexual preference, etc. I fill out my name and other matters as requested. Under the heading Sexual Preference, for example, I check "Queer," one of a few options printed on the form.

The first few minutes of our session are spent going over the form together. When she gets to the section labeled Sexual Preference, she stops. "Queer?" she says out loud. "What is that supposed to mean?"

"It is one of the options on your form," I say, perplexed. Then I add, "People use it to describe a sexuality that isn't based on gender," in case her question was sincere and she doesn't know what the word means.

"Do you date men or women?" she demands.

"Uh, I date . . . whoever I want to?" I respond.

"So, women," she says, making a note on my form. "I'll just put 'Gay/Lesbian.'"

———

A man I meet online invites me for a drink and I agree to meet him, although I am skeptical we will get along because he has the physical aspect of a drummer—tall and lanky, with a gaze that is watchful but self-absorbed. He expresses concern that he might drink too much to drive home but immediately orders a drink, and then another a few minutes later. He tells me about his band, which he does, indeed, drum in, and verbally urges me to "like" his Facebook page. He asks me no questions. When I finish my glass of wine, I tell him that I'm done for the night and prepare to leave.

"But wait," he says. "You didn't even tell me what you do!"

"I'm a writer," I say.

"Cool," he says, bobbing his head up and down. "Car manuals?"

———

In line at the drugstore, I am carrying a bottle of detergent. The man in front of me is close to my age and smiling at everyone in line. He takes particular interest in my detergent, asking how much it costs, exclaiming that he uses the same kind, and telling me how much it costs at another store, where he usually buys it. He manages to talk to me about laundry detergent for about five minutes, and I suspect that he is gearing up to get more personal, even though I work hard to cultivate disinterest in the line at the pharmacy. What is there to talk about, health problems? How understaffed the facility is? How expensive prescription drugs are? The health care system in America? Nothing good can come out of a conversation in line at the pharmacy. Yet he persists in this conversation about laundry detergent. I cannot escape, because I am out of the medication I am picking up today and need to take it immediately, although I do glance around in mild panic. After a brief pause following his final utterance about my three-dollar bottle of liquid soap, he says, "So, you married?"

"I'm not interested," I blurt out immediately, cutting off his question.

———

When you are not in it, you quickly forget the peculiar effects of depression. You breathe with full lung capacity, your mind does not ping back and forth between two annoying subjects, you call friends without concern that you will displease them, you eat when hungry. Feeling normal is in all ways unremarkable; in fact, it is the state of feeling nothing remarkable and failing to remark upon it. When a friend asks how you are and you say "fine" without thinking about it, you are brushing off the question, although you are also honoring unremarkability by moving on to subjects about which there is more to say. When depressed, the world constricts. All you can really do is think, I am depressed, or I hate myself, or something similar.

———

I try a new therapist and explain that I have had a difficult year. She gives me a sympathetic smile. By way of introduction, she tells me she lives in a suburb and has two kids. She has long blond hair and is slightly overweight. She is white. I tell her about my attempts to date, my seemingly constant harassment by men in public, my sense of isolation in my otherwise delightful neighborhood. I tell her about the man I met while on assignment who had pursued me romantically and then suddenly, angrily, severed contact. The therapist does not prod me for details. Instead she gives me a knowing look that indicates she already knows what's going on. "Is it the Blacks?" she says warmly. At first I find it odd, because in fact all of my most difficult interactions in the city have been with white folks. The story I have just told her, in fact, is about a white man. I consider clarifying this. Then I think I will ask her to explain herself. When I finally open my mouth, no words come out. So I leave.

———

I receive an email out of the blue from a man I care about dearly but who hurt me some years beforehand. He owes me something, he says, an explanation. He tells me then why he hurt me, but within his explanation is the assurance that he will hurt me again. Then he asks if I want to try over. I say why not.

This turns out to be a mistake.

———

When the shooting at the Pulse nightclub happens, one of the neighbor girls comes over to ask if I heard about what happened in Orlando.

"I did," I tell her. "What do you think about it?"

"We want you to know that Muslims aren't like that," she says. It isn't clear if she is speaking on behalf of the actual, invisible, neighborhood council that convenes occasionally to determine certain aspects of my life—do I require a gate around my

AC unit in the back, for example, or am I gardening correctly and in a pleasing manner?—or if she is utilizing the royal "we" to be fancy.

I proceed slowly. "Well, I know that is not what *you* are like, but people do ask me sometimes what it's like to live in a majority-Muslim community." I do not add "as a queer person," because it's not yet clear if this is a conversation about Muslim people not being inherently violent or queer people feeling safe. Instead I ask, "Do you know very many gay or lesbian Muslim people?" My intention is to suggest that she does know queer people who are not Muslim.

She rears her head back as if I have taken this whole conversation in a totally unexpected direction. "There aren't any," she says with finality, after a pause. Then she changes the subject and, soon, leaves.

———

In Cambodia, I am at first told that strict gender roles discourage gender and sexual diversity and that it would be unsafe for me to be out as a queer person while traveling alone in the country. This is quickly revealed to be bunk, although I do refrain from actively discussing my sexuality while I am living in an all-girl college dormitory with young women from the provinces. I also fail to share too many details of what, exactly, I am up to when I go out at night, and I never mention to my young Cambodian friends when I spend an evening at a lesbian bar or a drag show or organizing alongside transgender sex workers.

I do, however, let the young women read my work. And when one of the young women picks up on the queer themes tucked inside a language manual I wrote and brought along with me, I see that she has found something new and important. I watch as she lets it seep into her interests and, later, inform her identity. A decade later she has married her girlfriend and heads an international LGBTQ+ organization.

———

I go on occasional dates with women but these are unremarkable. I wonder often if it is a symptom of queer femme invisibility that I am more private about my relationships with women, that I protect them from public view, that I remain unsure about them for longer, that they hover on the fringes of other kinds of relationships sometimes indefinitely. I do know that what I believe relationships look like is based largely on my parents, and this concerns me deeply.

———

Another year in Detroit passes, during which I make few friends, lose a pet, struggle financially, find and then lose again a significant relationship, and suffer other standard life-related woes. I visit a third therapist. I believe her job is to help me make the best of my circumstances and that she will assist me in navigating what I have been calling "a bad patch."

"Leave," she says instead. "You don't belong here."

———

What turns out to be my last date in Detroit is bad. It is with a scientist who works on color. He tells me he developed a theory during his studies that transparency isn't simply a color variable, as in, objects could be red, green, yellow, or transparent, but that object opacity itself is a product of light quality, as is color. His lab tested the theory by finding the exact variety of light required to turn certain objects transparent: an orange, for example, or a bluet. He explains this to me over several expensive glasses of wine and I am riveted, even as I see that I will not sleep with him. What I realize is that color isn't merely a matter of light; opacity itself is—the attribute we most rely on to determine objecthood. There's something monumental to the discovery that the visual qualities we use to assess a thing's volume, weight, endurance, and potential are only a trick of light and may shift under the right conditions.

What I am saying is that I learn on this date that it is possible to see through anything. Anything at all. The date is bad, but my whole perspective changes.

———

One morning I am planting lavender in the front garden when Nishat and Sadia come running over to me, very excited. They act as if they have a secret, like the day they looked me up on the internet and then asked extremely specific questions about my life to indicate their extensive knowledge of my biography. "Anne!

Anne!" they yell, crowding around me, as if there were several of each of them.

"What are you two up to?" I ask.

They exchange a look and take a breath. "Happy Queer Visibility Day!" they shout together, waving their arms.

4

THE CITY

Great bodies of people are never responsible for what they do. They are driven by instincts which are not in their control. . . . True, they had money and power, but only at the cost of harboring in their breasts an eagle, a vulture, for ever tearing the liver out and plucking at the lungs—the instinct for possession, the rage for acquisition which drives them to desire other people's fields and goods perpetually; to make frontiers and flags; battleship and poison gas; to offer up their own lives and their children's lives.

—VIRGINIA WOOLF, *A Room of One's Own*

I am in Finland during the winter, so even though it is lunchtime, we are having a fire in the twilight with people from the local village. One villager, a man approximately my age who has never left Finland, engages me in conversation although he speaks little English. I gather he is a farmer, perhaps of sheep, who likes gangster movies and prefers to keep up with American television only when it is dubbed into Finnish, which can take decades. He wants to know about *The Sopranos*, a program about which he has heard many positive things. Are they true? I cannot say. I explain that I am a writer and prefer books, and he counters with the information that he does not read books. He reads, he says, "some websites." He does not specify whether they are news sites, whether he reads certain websites consistently, or whether he only reads online sources under duress when reading is, for some reason, necessary. He does not distinguish one website from another in any way.

Conversation, stilted at first, begins to drag. He asks where I am from, and I explain that I recently moved from Chicago to Detroit.

"Ah," he says knowingly, his enthusiasm mounting. "Detroit! The only interesting city in America." He goes on to describe the city's bankruptcy, poverty, corruption, and continuing decline.

———

According to World Population Review, the population of Detroit in 2019 is approximately 672,662, a decline from 2010's 713,777 and a drastic decline from 2000's 951,270. At its peak in the 1950s, the population was twice that. The racial demographics over this time have also shifted, and the city currently boasts a 79.2 percent Black population; 14.1 percent white population; 1.5 percent Asian population; 0.34 percent Native American population; 0.02 percent Native Hawaiian or Pacific Islander population; and 4.92 percent other or mixed-race population.

———

My internet goes out again, four months after the last outage. This time the internet service provider does not send a service tech. They don't even bother calling me back to tell me when service will resume, even though they promise to whenever I call, which I do every single day. After five days I get the hint and cancel my service. During this same week, there are street repairs at both ends of my block, and for two days I can neither drive anywhere nor go online. The nearest grocery store is 1.7 miles away.

———

When Detroit incorporates as a city in 1806, it is only a square mile in size, but it grows. By 1889, it is fast approaching the southern borders of the cities now known as Hamtramck and Highland Park. Both Hamtramck and Highland Park, around that time, decide to shore up local government, ensuring that they will not be swallowed up in the growing city of Detroit by incorporating as distinct villages. In Hamtramck, this decision is due to the active and robust Polish and German communities that see a future for their village; Highland Park, on the other hand, is led by a rich real estate magnate, and it is unclear what benefit he sees in the action. Nonetheless, by 1908, the Michigan state constitution enacts the Home Rule Cities Act, allowing local municipalities increased say over their futures. Although Detroit is now actively trying to annex the two villages, Henry Ford, who'd purchased land in Highland Park for a Model T complex, and the Dodge brothers, who plan to build the Poletown plant in Hamtramck, don't want to pay Detroit tax rates and rally for continued independence. When the villages then incorporate into cities, the debate about annexation is over.

In this way we can say that Detroit was quite literally shaped by the auto industry. Or we can call it corporate greed.

————

I volunteer at an urban farm and distribute seed packets at a membership event. A woman with a commanding presence runs the sign-in table. As new arrivals enter the room, they line up at her station, and after a nice, long line has formed, she throws her arms wide and announces cheerily, "Welcome to Wakanda!" She is referencing the utopic African nation from *Black Panther*, a film that has just been released. I am standing directly to her left and when she sees me, she appears to notice that I am white, one of few white people, perhaps the only one, in the room. She squares her gaze in my direction. "Wakanda," she says directly to me, "is for everybody."

————

A woman emails me because she hears I have been asking about local literacy programs. In her email she writes that she presumes I own many books. She would like some, she says. She is taking up donations because her child's school library does not have any books. She says this casually, as if books were an option that this library simply chose not to offer. Later I discover it is common in Detroit schools to not have books. I give her every title I can spare.

————

A faraway friend has purchased tickets to the symphony for my birthday, so one day in the spring, a local pal and I get dressed up and meet at an outdoor café before the concert. The neighborhood, Cass Corridor, can be described as rapidly developing, rapidly gentrifying, or rapidly deteriorating, depending on who is speaking. During our meal, a woman walks by and begins muttering loudly to her friend about how she has lived in the neighborhood for years and is appalled by recent changes. She gesticulates performatively toward the restaurant. A young white woman, a café patron, seated with several other young white women a few tables away from us, laughs rudely at her performance. The woman from the neighborhood, older and Black, becomes enraged.

The host of the establishment, a burly man, emerges, and the neighborhood woman speaks to him in an angered but reasonable tone. "You act white," she says, "but I know your mama. How are you OK making money from all this?"

The host tells her to leave. Instead she puts the question to him again, louder. This time he shoves her, hard, and she stumbles and falls backward into the street. When she gets up, he punches her in the face.

———

I am contracted by a news outlet to collaborate with an illustrator on a monthly comics journalism strip on Detroit residents' struggles with land, housing, and water rights. It is also a way for me to call up amazing, thoughtful, local activists and spend time with them, and in this way I meet Alice Jennings, the civil rights attorney involved in many of the most pressing water rights lawsuits of the decade, who works in the Cadillac building downtown. Water shutoffs in Detroit are contracted out to a company called Homrich Wrecking, Inc., the company that turned off water services to approximately one hundred thousand Detroit homes over bill nonpayment before the city drastically shifted gears following a wrist slap from the United Nations. Homrich Wrecking, a demolition service that also does teardowns, has offices in the Cadillac building too, just around the corner from Jennings's office. "Makes my blood boil every time I get off the elevator!" Jennings tells me, her eyes wide.

———

The empty lot at the end of the block across the street that we use as a local dump is suddenly a bustle of activity. Men in matching outfits come and clear away the concrete rubble that has fallen around the entryway and that I had been stealing to build a path through my garden. They trim all the trees back—formerly mulberry bushes, now strong and thick enough to require chainsaws—and leave the wall protected by an ineffective row of stumps. They clear all the dumped material away, which the city has never done. The concrete structure is emptied of debris and cleaned, and the yard before it is made even and neat.

The neighborhood is abuzz. "What will happen there?" I ask the neighbor girls.

"It will be a community center," Sadia says. But it sits untouched for a long time, and debris again accumulates.

———

The ubiquitous phrase "Say nice things about Detroit" is coined during Detroit's most difficult days by an entrepreneurial white woman named Emily Gail who runs a series of small gift shops in the 1970s and '80s. According to *Crain's Detroit Business*, the phrase first appears on a banner trailing behind a plane Gail rents for four hundred dollars while vacationing in Florida. "We kept running into people we knew from Michigan," Gail tells reporter Ariel Black for the August 26, 2015, story. "They'd say, 'Aren't you glad you're out of Detroit?' We weren't, because we had a business there and were pumping it up."

The phrase then emerges on T-shirts, pins, and bumper stickers, available at her shops, and Gail publicizes her merchandise and its underlying concept with a series of runs through the streets of downtown just as white flight to the suburbs peaks. Her business, however, fails, even as other businesses return to the downtown area. In 2015, she lives in Hawaii, and the phrase has been revived by high-end watchmaker Shinola upon the company's much-touted move from Brooklyn and picked up by a handful of other local businesses.

Gail's approach to this co-optation is initially friendly and welcoming, asking businesses who use the phrase to simply attach her name to it. (When Whole Foods emblazons it on a wall without her permission, for example, she is later asked to add her signature.) But in 2018, she trademarks the name and enlists lawyers to ensure no one uses it except certain licensed merchandisers. "I need to pay for my trips here," Gail, now seventy-two, tells reporter Neal Rubin for a July 17, 2018, article in *The Detroit News*.

———

I grow to love the city's sense of interior architecture, largely based on a never-quite-finished version of modernism, as if we were all invited to a Henri Matisse exhibition but, once drunk, urged to hang the paintings ourselves and offered no training in museum installation techniques. Spaces often feel like a Frank Gehry badly damaged in a long-ago air raid or not yet completed. I paint three walls of my living room a dark blue but, tired, let the final wall sit, only one-third painted, for over a year. No one complains; in fact, I receive more than a few compliments. Modernist furniture, which really did emerge from nearby Grand Rapids, is readily available, as are objects culled from the factories of Albert Kahn, many illegally. Most houses exist in an incomplete state, and it is not unusual to sit on an overturned bucket at a fancy dinner party or to move tubes of sealant out of the way to put wine down for guests. The interior spaces of the city are perfectly congruous with the exterior spaces, buildings torn open by fire but still standing and new constructions that run out of funding. Backyard gardens that maybe someday will be installed but for now are just large piles of dirt or gravel or used plywood; public schools with exterior scaffolding, allowing for ongoing repairs. Michigan is the place where modernism was born and then died. In Detroit it is both mourned and honored, given space to exist as a good idea that failed.

Virginia Woolf is one of modernism's greatest success stories. Her essay "Modern Fiction" sought to define the literary era, a queen knighting her most worthy subjects, and *A Room of One's*

Own stands as something of a modernist feat. In it, she dwells on her thoughts, and her thoughts about her thoughts. She endeavors to describe these thoughts "fully and freely." That she believes herself capable of a full range of thought and free expansiveness within it is a characteristic of modernism; today, informed by several waves of feminist thought, critical race theory, and the Black Lives Matter movement, we would be more likely to acknowledge the notion that thoughts are limited by experience. It is for this reason that writers tend to identify themselves in text—"As a well-traveled white queer cis woman with disabilities raised upper-middle class," etc.—and indeed why the concept of identity politics exists and, as well, gets derided. It can be a lot to constantly position oneself before presenting one's views, to remain vigilant against claims of authority that can so easily crumble. There are those who cling to the authority modernism allows for, the hierarchies it creates. But, generally speaking, they do not live in Detroit.

———

I go to an event intended to galvanize local neighborhood concerns into a platform proposal for a local politician, the kind of thing where you consume fruit and bagels and coffee and then do a lot of "breakout sessions" and "brainstorming." "There are no bad ideas!" That sort of thing.

There are no Bengalis in the room, but I have asked my neighbors what they might like me to bring to such a session, and so most of what I bring to the table represents their interests: that city offices make Bangla translators available, that the city formally adopt sanctuary city status and stop sharing immigration status with Immigration and Customs Enforcement, that meetings like this offer childcare so they can personally attend, that the schools stop scheduling exams during Ramadan, when the children are fasting. When the conversation turns to community accountability, and what measures might be put in place to track the progress of our requests, I speak as a journalist.

"It would be great if city council meetings were transcribed and made available online," I suggest. And "what I would love to see, as a journalist, is a designated individual in direct communication with elected officials, who can respond to questions."

A businesswoman at the table interrupts me. "I'm sorry," she says. "You're a journalist? I'm going to have to ask you to leave."

I am surprised and explain that I am not covering the event, just stating what would help me ensure access to information. I am sure I misunderstood her, that she did not just ask me to leave a public meeting because of my profession.

"Yes, but you could," she says. "You could write about this. I have a business to protect. You need to leave."

So I leave.

———

Other initiatives arise to offer free houses in the Motor City. In 2016, Ramzu Yunus, a leader in the African American sovereignty movement, holds an event in Highland Park for Black Independence Day. He offers attendees a cash payment and a free house. Approximately three hundred people gather at Highland Park city hall and, reports say, become agitated; police are called and Yunus arrested. Two years later, Yunus again offers free houses to Detroiters, this time in exchange for a signature on a petition calling for an independent government. It's part of what he calls the Detroit Free Housing Program, which he claims is backed by the city. Yunus's group attracts hundreds to the Coleman A. Young Municipal Center in downtown Detroit on July 4, 2018, as Charles Ramirez explains in *The Detroit News* that day.

"You're talking about housing, which is a critical issue, especially decent, quality and affordable housing, in the city," Detroit City Council president pro tem Mary Sheffield tells Ramirez. "It's unfortunate whoever organized the event led people on with the belief they will receive a home. Housing is a sensitive topic for many people."

———

The downtown public library is grand and stately, although I hope you are not reading this book for sightseeing tips. Inside are frescoes, rotting, ornate decorations marred by water stains or holes, and a display of all the former branches of the Detroit Public Library system, their years of and reasons for closure or, in a few cases, their current hours. The main branch is not open on Sundays, and then it opens on Sundays. For three years, the branch near my house is not open when I stop by. I go to the main branch instead to request information on the history of my neighborhood, but the librarian looks annoyed when I ask for assistance. He tells me there are no books for me. So I leave.

———

Ethnographer James C. Scott makes a compelling case, in his book on the Malaysian village he lived in for two years in the late 1970s, *Weapons of the Weak: Everyday Forms of Peasant Resistance*, that people stripped of what we traditionally consider power assert themselves politically by alternative means. Deliberately economically disadvantaged folks, he explains, or those who have scant access to government decision-making processes, thus exert a sort of political power by showing up late or feigning ignorance. In great numbers, Scott describes, such individual acts of foot-dragging and noncompliance can have a cumulative effect, resulting in a slow-moving transfer of power from those who have to those who have not.

My enthusiasm for the strategy flags when my basement floods with sewage and the plumber arrives three days late.

———

Liana, Casey, and I meet regarding the organization, from which communications have begun to arrive inconsistently. We discuss in distressed tones that the organization has not yet put Nandi in the house that was now promised to her over a year earlier. As the only Detroiter chosen for the program, it feels urgent that she be able to move into her house as soon as possible, although the first house purchased for her has been discovered to have structural flaws. We realize that what each of us has been told about the program is inconsistent, and there are further inconsistencies within each house that seem odd. Liana, for example, has both a second floor and a washing machine; I have neither. She and I were both given Spirit of Detroit Awards but Casey was not. These are oddities, and we discuss them only in terms of how we will shape the program going forward, as we come into legal ownership of our homes and join the board: we agree to stipulate certain baseline requirements per house and clearly share with incoming winners what amenities each house has in advance so confusion is avoided. Nandi's house, however, remains our foremost concern. If the program is looking for houses to purchase and renovate now, how long will it be before she is settled in her home. Another year?

———

In the backyard, suddenly there are kittens. Under zucchini leaves, mewling in the strawberry patch, sunning themselves on concrete. The neighbor children name the tabbies Thurber II and Thurber III, the black cats Metal Van II and Metal Van III. There are also kittens of other colors but my young friends don't know what to call them. For my smallest neighbors, the city is a vast unknown, best when populated by friends.

———

Property taxes in my first year of residence are a little over $1,200. In my second year, I publish a comic that looks at Detroit's famously high property tax rates, and it is well read, viral. My next property tax bill is twenty-four dollars.

———

A video circulates online, days after the 2016 presidential election, that depicts white students taunting students of color by chanting "Build the wall!" in a suburban school. "This was a particularly contentious campaign cycle, with words and actions that, arguably, our youngest students should not have witnessed," writes the superintendent of Birmingham Public Schools Dr. Daniel Nerad, according to a November 11, 2016, *Detroit Free Press* article.

"Sadia, are you having any problems like this at your school?" I ask.

"Oh, no," she says. "There aren't that many white kids at my school."

———

"I don't think I've ever lived in a city that talks about itself as much as Detroit," a local artist confesses in wonder over drinks one night. It's true. At parties, in bars, at restaurants: most conversations in the city are devoted to the subject of the city. Political speeches by both officials and activists open on Detroit's oft-celebrated hustle, grit, or "people," although few specifics are ever offered. The boosterism is widespread but thin. There are several varieties of shirt that you can buy, for example, that proclaim nothing whatsoever about the city except for its name.

———

In 2011, it is announced that nearly half the population of the city of Detroit—47 percent—is functionally illiterate. There is a public backlash, naysaying, and much debunking, and then the world moves on to other concerns. In 2018, the Detroit Public Schools Community District scores lowest among all urban districts in the country on math and reading in a National Assessment of Educational Progress (NAEP) report; only 7 percent of the eighth-grade students tested at or above the NAEP proficient reading level. These are the worst scores in the test's forty-year history, a problem compounded by the district's lowest graduation rate in the country that year.

Jamarria Hall, who graduates from Osborn High School in 2017 at the top of his class, two years later joins six other students in a lawsuit against the school district, in which the students argue that their fundamental right to literacy has been denied. Hall describes moldy smells throughout hallways, dead rodents in bathrooms, water leaks from ceilings into buckets or onto students' heads during classes. He tells *The Detroit News* on October 22, 2019, that during his school years, teachers often failed to show up for class, that there were no textbooks, and that students were habitually sent to the gym to watch movies. The students' case argues that young people in public educational systems have a constitutional right to literacy, which leads to an embarrassment of public officials and political leaders making grand statements to the contrary.

In April 2020, a federal court affirms that Detroit public school students have a fundamental right to literacy. Nearly $100 million is awarded the plaintiffs and literacy programs for the Detroit Public Schools Community District, although schools are at the time closed for the pandemic.

———

During the fiftieth anniversary of the 1967 uprisings, I visit an exhibition at the city historical museum. I am reading a display about Ossian Sweet's house, pictured in the exhibition because Sweet, a Black doctor, had purchased a house in a white Detroit neighborhood in 1925. An angry mob formed, a man was shot, and Clarence Darrow defended Sweet in court against charges of murder. Eventually acquitted, Sweet's story acts as a reminder of the long history of racial segregation in the city and the role that homeowning and placemaking have in the events of '67. This history is mostly frustrating, filled with restrictive housing covenants and border walls between neighborhoods, incidents of arson and beatings and murder. The man standing next to me turns to share that he grew up across the street from Ossian Sweet's house in the 1960s and always read a hope for change in the man's tale. "Ah," the now-grown man tells me, as we stroll together past the displays at the heart of the exhibition, the section devoted to the five-day riots. "The free store," he says, chuckling at a reconstruction of a storefront being looted. "They always forget to mention how much fun we had." He flashes me a charming grin.

I feel lucky to meet someone who reminds me to look for joy in the city's history.

———

Friends come to visit from out of town and I take them to all my favorite spots in the city: Caribbean Citchen, MotorCity Wine, Yemen Café, Royal Kabob, Rose's Fine Food, Louisiana Creole Gumbo, the Pink Flamingo, Aladdin Sweets and Café, the Royce Detroit, and eventually, Marrow. I construct our outings carefully, driving by or stopping at the MBAD African Bead Museum, Hamtramck Disneyland, the Packard Plant, the Guardian Building, the Heidelberg Project, and sites no longer standing: the Algiers Motel, large swaths of the Jefferson-Chalmers neighborhood, plots of land just north of my house recently purchased en masse by shipping and transportation billionaire Matty Moroun for unclear purposes. Even friends familiar with the violence a municipal government can wreak are stunned by what Detroit residents face daily, by the leveled blank spaces between houses and behind restaurants. "I don't think I could do it," one says flatly.

———

Sadia is home on a weekday morning, and I ask her why she's not in school. "The water," she says and shrugs. During a subsequent internet search I discover there is a boil advisory in the city, and we are not supposed to drink water from the tap until further notice, although residents have received no notification. Sadia returns to school four days later. She is never warned against drinking from the water fountains, although water bottles are suddenly issued to each student.

———

It is the end of the workday and I am stuck at the exit of a parking structure after my physical therapy session has ended. The machine will not take my credit card, so the gate will not open, and eight cars are lined up behind me, honking and becoming angry that I am blocking the exit, but I cannot move my car without busting through the unopened gate. The only option I have is to press a small button that says HELP and wait to see what happens. Seven minutes later, more cars have joined the line behind me. A woman about three cars back opens her window and screams, "Can't somebody just swipe her through? It's not like we actually expect these machines to work. We do this every day!" Whereupon someone in the car in front of her gets out, scuttles up to the machine, and swipes their employee ID. The gate opens. I leave.

———

The mayor announces that the city will resume street cleaning. A few months later, signs do, indeed, appear around the neighborhood: NO PARKING. STREET CLEANING. THURSDAY, 9:00

A.M. TO 4:00 P.M. So Wednesday night, I park on a different block. Walking to my house I see that my neighbors have chosen a different interpretation of the sign. They are parked on lawns, front yards, empty lots, the sidewalk. A cacophony of tan and beige minivans: Suzukis, Nissans, Hondas. Parked where people usually go.

The street cleaners never arrive. Eventually, the neighborhood returns to normal.

———

One day I see a young girl, maybe four years old, holding a closed umbrella. She is frowning, holding one end of the umbrella in her right hand, repeatedly beating it into her left palm, except the umbrella is so large in her tiny hands that she can barely grasp it. She looks angry, but stands a ways off from anyone, alone, staring at a corner of the sidewalk. She's beating the umbrella into her palm like a cop threatening a perp, and frowning very, very hard—glowering—but at nothing that I can see. I realize that she has watched a man in her life do this, many times.

———

Ramadan is coming and the girls are talking outfits. This year, almost the entirety of Ramadan will be held while school is in session, and students are expected to take exams shortly before Eid, after they have been fasting for several weeks.

"It's so unfair!" Nishat complains.

"Isn't it also a violation of your constitutional rights?" I ask. "I think you're supposed to be allowed to celebrate religious holidays without harassment from the state."

The next year exams are again scheduled during the last days of Ramadan, and Sadia organizes a petition for Muslim students to be allowed makeup exams after Ramadan has ended. The petition is ignored. The following year exams are again scheduled during Ramadan.

————

I come to suspect that the Thirty-Sixth District Court, where I must go every day for the first two weeks of February, is nothing more than a low-level parking-meter scam. Among standard prohibited items—alcohol, box cutters, brass knuckles, food and beverages, guns, and knives—I am not allowed to bring my cell phone inside. I am in attendance to follow court proceedings involving a group of water rights activists arrested for disrupting Homrich Wrecking's water shutoffs. I can bring pens and pencils and paper with me, although no pencil sharpeners or markers, but because my pen is deemed a marker and confiscated, and my autoimmune diseases limit my ability to grasp writing implements anyway, the concession does me little good. More distressing, I must load up on parking in advance, which in Detroit is managed via app, since I can't take my cell phone inside to reload the meter once my time runs out. The app allows a maximum of two hours' parking, and cases are often delayed by or run over two hours, at which point I have to leave the courtroom to move my car or virtually plug the meter from my car, where I have stored my cell phone. Little to no information about ongoing cases is available inside the facility.

My case is delayed many times and then, while I am out re-loading the parking meter, rescheduled entirely, information I am only alerted to the following morning, via text from one of the defendants. Since I can take few notes inside the facility even if I happen to be present when information is offered, I quickly begin to wonder why the public is allowed entry to the Thirty-Sixth District Court at all. I come away with no relevant information in two weeks' time but do spend eighteen dollars on parking.

———

My comics journalism project brings me to Nicole Hill, who first sounded the alarm when Detroit began shutting off water ser-vices to an estimated seventy thousand homes during a two-year period starting in 2014. In a situation that, years later, is revealed to have been initiated by a billing error, she loses running water in her home, which causes an immediate array of difficulties in-comprehensible in an industrialized nation. "I had not been able to properly sanitize my house or stay hydrated," she tells me. The lack of running water also worsens her health problems imme-diately. "The way the doctor described it was like, when you get dehydrated, your insides turn dry, and it cracks. Literally any-thing can just creep in there." She borrows water from neighbors and, as she brings attention to the problem to local, national, and international audiences—linking the cause to the poisoned water of nearby Flint—survives off donated water from a spate of aid initiatives.

For two months, her life is horrific, she says. She eliminates water from food preparation and fries everything, gaining forty or fifty pounds. Water salvaged from clothes washing, dishes, and bathing is used to flush the toilet. Other uses are abandoned. Mopping the floor is out, because water used for such purposes is going to evaporate, is nonrecoverable. Her asthma worsens, she tells me, when she stops drinking water.

The story of the water shutoffs in Detroit, which target poor communities of color but ignore corporations owing millions in unpaid water bills, is one of incredible cruelty. It is easy to look at a map of the affected areas and perceive an agenda behind the shutoffs involving the seizure of land and evacuation of the poor. But it is less easy to grasp how difficult it is to live without running water in the United States in the twenty-first century.

When I request the city shut off my water while I travel for the winter, I am told the Detroit Water and Sewerage Department will not make advance appointments for shutoffs, will only complete them sometime within two days after you call. I store four times as much water as I think I might need, and then call, and my water is shut off within hours, leaving me without running water for two days. I wash my hands regularly and don't cut out drinking water. But the dishes never get fully clean, and the bathroom goes unscrubbed. I do not mop, either.

Still, I do OK until the night before I am to leave town, when I spill food on the floor. I clear out my remaining water supply cleaning it up, but then I have nothing to wash my hands with and can no longer flush the toilet. I drive to a friend's house to borrow three gallons of tap water to get through the night. This is deeply humiliating.

―――――

"It may seem like a small thing to you but for the people in this city who are thinking, 'I'm getting tired of living here, maybe I'll move out,' that street sweeper coming down the street says the quality of life is really being restored," Mayor Mike Duggan tells *The New York Times* on April 30, 2018.

―――――

Do I need to explain that there aren't snowplows? Or, worse, that there are some but that they don't visit my neighborhood? That during snowstorms the men on the block who have jobs stay with friends in neighborhoods where snowplows do come or pay a Bengali man a few streets away with a plow on the front of his pickup to clear a path to the highway?

―――――

The psychovisual effect of living in a city from which entire blocks of housing have been swiped clean with no traces left of the people that once inhabited the area is stunning. Perhaps more jarring are the blocks with only one or two houses left standing, a reminder that people do still exist in the environment, although far fewer than in days past. Where did they go? Why did they leave? What am I still doing here? Are we in danger? People shorthand this feeling with phrases like "bombed out" and "war zone" but the post-conflict nations I've spent time in bustle with activity, eager to heal and repair, and facilities are established and supported to ensure survival and potential. In former war zones I often feel engaged, alert, abuzz. In Detroit I am usually left with a sense of awe, as if in the aftermath of a municipally specific rapture.

———

I return from Europe and go to the bank to exchange and deposit my remaining euros, but the bank teller can't figure out what country they are from. "They're euros," I explain. "They're a currency a lot of countries in Europe use." She doesn't believe me. Eventually she tells me I should try again on a different day, preferably when she isn't working. Then she leans in toward the window and, in a lowered voice, promises not to tell anyone the bills are obviously fake.

———

A friend and I attend the evening performance of an artist acquaintance. We have been warned that the performance is emotional, as it concerns race in America. Indeed, the audience is invited to perform a small ritual in public mourning of Black men lost to violence at the hands of police. Approximately eight audience members perform the ritual in turn. Each performance takes nearly five minutes, during which time the sun sets, casting first a golden, then blue, hue over the proceedings. Once the sun has set and we are enshrouded in darkness, the artist takes out a Bible and begins to read a passage from it. A brief Bible study ensues. My friend and I look at each other with raised eyebrows but stay until the group breaks up. We are not Christians, but we do not have any other plans.

―――――

"Inoperable boilers. Corroded plumbing fixtures. Missing ceiling tiles in classrooms. Exterior walls with cracks. Roof leaks. Incomplete fire alarm systems. Electrical panels in classrooms known to be fire hazards," Jennifer Chambers catalogs the immediate necessary repairs required at over one hundred Detroit public schools for *The Detroit News* on April 30, 2019.

―――――

Two years after the lot across the street was cleared, it has once again filled with discarded home goods, broken furniture, pallets, tires, and used lumber. "I guess there will be no community center," Sadia says sadly. Then the men in matching outfits reappear and again haul away the refuse. They retrim the stumps, clear the concrete structure of accumulated debris, and yell back and forth to one another. They park two large dumpsters on the land, as if to say, This is where garbage goes now.

But the dumpsters are tall, and we cannot see what is inside them, so the corner loses its distinction as a community reuse facility. We still remove objects from our homes that no longer hold value, but once they are in the dumpster we cannot see what others have left. No one stops by to see what has accumulated, no one grabs a bit of wood to fix their back step, no one finds a fan that someone else had discarded but that works perfectly, even if it is a little loud.

If there is to be a community center here, it is not clear which community will be welcome in it.

———

While I am away for several weeks, the Detroit Water and Sewerage Department charges me nearly five hundred dollars for water usage, more than five times what I am charged during a normal month. Usage, their reports indicate, was particularly heavy during a forty-eight-hour period during which there was no one in my home, when nearly four hundred dollars' worth of water usage was generated. When I call to question the bill, I am asked to remember whether those were the days that I filled my swimming pool or let all my taps run full blast for forty-eight hours. My answers, that I do not own a swimming pool and that I was traveling during the two days in question and am not in the habit of letting my taps run full blast for any period of time, elicit no response. Neither does my follow-up explanation that there are no unusual leaks or evidence of water in my home to indicate any great volume of usage, nor indeed any usage at all. Somehow, the worker I am speaking to fails to note in my file that I am disputing nearly five hundred dollars in water charges, and the following month they appear, again, and now include a late fee. When I call to check on the status of my ongoing dispute, I am told that it was never filed and that I have now missed the deadline to dispute the bill and must pay it immediately or lose service. I am offered a payment plan to spread payments over the next six months, although I must agree never to complain about the charge again. "By entering into this Agreement, Customer waives the right to dispute responsibility for the arrearage, as well as any right to a hearing as to the validity of the arrearage," the agreement states.

———

For a while I save what I dig up in my garden. A gallery of the most elaborate stumps, small toys, and electronic gadgets unearthed from the soil. Buried in the depths of the dirt is an entire floor's worth of laminate, which I pick out, brush off, and reconfigure on the concrete in the backyard. Dumping, it turns out, incurs costs that most contractors are unwilling to cover, so often teardowns or discarded building materials are just abandoned in neighborhood lots or dumped into backyards and covered over with dirt.

———

"How likely are you to recommend Detroit Public Schools Community District to a friend or family member or as a place to work?" asks a survey that Superintendent Nikolai Vitti unveiled in June 2018 at a board of education meeting. The *Free Press*, on June 14, prints a few responses. Forty percent of families say they "wouldn't recommend the district"; 50 percent of teaching staff agree, as does 63 percent of administrative staff.

———

New street-cleaning signs. Not everyone takes them seriously this time. Some do, resuming a commitment to parking on the sidewalk or lawn when warned against parking on the street. A man drives across my front yard, murdering two young juneberry saplings, to get to the yard he has decided to park on. No amount of explaining will get him to understand that I do not want him to drive on my lawn.

Late in the day, the street-sweeping truck arrives. No one can believe it! It sweeps up so much dust that a thin fog settles into the neighborhood, and the quality of light becomes unusual, special. It sweeps in sum exactly one side of the street, although it is supposed to return to do the other side, and thus clears away only a portion of the trash accumulated over the seven years since the street-sweeping trucks were retired from use. Also, since some disregard the signs, interpreting them as yet another administrative falsehood, the job the street sweepers do is spotty, leaving the pavement cleanish, wiping a meandering swath only where no cars are parked and only on the west side of the street. Anyway, this crooked sparkling path is filled in again moments later, once the dust resettles from its temporarily airborne state.

For a few moments, everyone is glued to front windows, like

they're glimpsing Santa Claus in action. Then for a few days, everyone is hopeful and alert.

———

To conduct interviews for my comics series, I visit an organization that offers assistance to Detroit residents facing foreclosure, which means I spend the day among desperate, out-of-luck people who, for the most part, are also extremely well organized. Diligent, thoughtful, engaging. Their primary failing seems to be that they do not understand tax law, which, what the hell, neither do I—who does?—but that isn't even why they had all, to a person, recently lost ownership of their homes, some that had been in their families for five or more generations. They had lost their homes because they do not have enough fucking money. That's all. There's no trick to it, no weirdness, no nuance. The story repeats in interview after interview. Three years ago something happened and they couldn't afford to pay their property taxes that year, and the next year they couldn't either, and then, third year, same deal. After three years: property tax foreclosure. Can you even imagine the terror that accumulates over those three years? I cannot. Now try to imagine living in a city where it happens to a quarter of the population.

———

"What's the biggest problem facing Detroit?" I ask Sadia one day. She has been reading the newspaper lately and is developing a sense of the city outside of our block, although she leaves the neighborhood infrequently.

"Our school has gas leaks. Sometimes it gets closed because of gas leaks. And the water is nasty. The ceiling is falling off, even though it is a new building. They remodeled it in, I think, 2012 or 2013," she scrunches up her face to remember. Her school is considered one of the best in the city.

But at least it's not her old school, she says. "With my old school we would have problems with flooding. The basement would flood. Preschoolers and kindergarteners have class in the basement. Then when I was in middle school our cafeteria flooded and we had to go home.

"Then we had a problem with the water. The water was coming out all gross and it smelled terrible. They made us stay the first day but then after that they sent us home until they fixed it. It was a couple days."

They did that with a gas leak, too, I recall. Kids were getting sick but the school wouldn't admit anything was wrong. "You got sick that day," I remind her. It was only a couple months prior.

"A lot of the teachers were getting sick and passing out," she recalls. After the teachers started falling ill, the school finally closed down. Sadia again expresses relief that her educational facilities have improved compared to her previous institution, but we become so engrossed in cataloging regular threats to her health and safety posed by her school that we fail to revisit the question of Detroit's biggest problem.

———

I develop a reputation as the best speaker of English on the block, so I am frequently consulted on obscure legal matters. It is soon determined, although for unclear reasons, that I am particularly skilled in the areas of property rights and immigration law, and so girls from several blocks away are apt to stop by and consult with me on their mother's citizenship test or the papers necessary to acquire the empty lot next door.

One of the young men across the street, a brother of Sadia, begins asking me about fences. I know nothing about fences, I tell him, but I can find out. I research building permit regulations and talk to neighbors, consult with professional fence installers. "OK," I tell him a few days later. "Here is what you must do."

After two days, the empty lot next to his house contains piles of wood. Then all the young men from the neighborhood start showing up at eight every morning and begin working together. There are so many young men in my neighborhood, I have never seen them all together! Working together for long hours, they complete the fence in three days. It is done late one Wednesday evening, and Sadia's brother is left alone with his project, stringing a row of lights across the very center of the fenced-in field, in the dark. Under it he installs two poles, and then a net between them, and then all the strapping young men from the neighborhood return. To play badminton.

5

THE WORK

So that when I ask you to earn money and have a room of your own, I am asking you to live in the presence of reality.

—VIRGINIA WOOLF, *A Room of One's Own*

In years past, my income has relied on my ability to travel for lectures, art projects, and the freelance stories I pick up from national outlets, but the organization requires that I spend 70 percent of my time in Detroit. In years that I release books, which has been most years for the last decade, the travel time this leaves is eaten up by book tours, lectures, and other promotional appearances. The restriction on my ability to travel is significant. Still, it is in some ways a relief. I look forward to finding local work that will tie me to this place and these people, although jobs, particularly in the arts, are difficult to come by in Detroit. One week I set up five networking meetings with five different professionals in my field—journalists, researchers, editors—one meeting per day, all with men. I clarify carefully that the intention of each meeting is to discuss local work opportunities. At each meeting except for one I am asked, eventually, for a date. At the meeting at which I am not asked for a date I am sexually propositioned in blunt language.

———

The general unemployment rate in Detroit is higher than that in other cities, with 5 percent in 2018, compared to New York's 4.1 percent and Seattle's 3.3 percent—however, these numbers are an improvement over the 28 percent unemployment rate in Detroit reported in 2009. Data from the Bureau of Labor Statistics suggests the unemployment rate drops a bit in 2019 in all areas except manufacturing, where it rises, although manufacturing continues to employ the fourth-highest number of people in the Detroit metro area, after the business sector; trade, transportation, and utilities; and education and health services. The data also shows costs of food rising in Detroit during this time, faster than the national average, and costs of utilities dropping, although much slower than the national average. During the previous year, housing prices per average income rose slightly, while discretionary spending and transportation costs fell. Since 2016, the unemployment rate has dropped by an average of 1 percent per year.

These last numbers fail to account for folks who are employed only part-time but would prefer full-time employment, and it doesn't tally those who have grown frustrated with the job search and are no longer looking for work. An expanded unemployment rate—usually running about twice standard unemployment rates—is considered by labor journalists to provide a more accurate depiction of unemployment numbers. Detroit, however, does not tally an expanded unemployment rate. The city has tallied an annual poverty rate since 2015, when nearly 40 percent of the city's families lived under the poverty line. In 2018, that number drops to 33.4 percent.

In other words, a third of the city lives under the poverty line, attributable to a lack of jobs and the high costs of food and housing.

———

After nearly a year I begin a short-term position teaching courses in art and design history, the field in which I hold a master's degree and have published several books. My students are challenging: They do not seem to like to read, appear uncomfortable with women in authority or the names of female historical figures, and rarely indicate any interests, in or outside of school. They occasionally complain after lectures that I am wrong, because they are experts in this or that area, while I know nothing because I have just begun teaching there. At the beginning of the semester, I introduce myself with my preferred pronouns and ask them to do the same, a practice not yet common at the institution, and several cis male students call me sexist and drop my class. None of this is all that surprising. It is the job of the student to challenge the teacher. It is not the students, however, who make the job difficult. On two occasions it is suggested that I change students' grades because parents have called in anger; I am urged to drop some of the women artists from my syllabus because too many unfamiliar names make students uncomfortable. In a teaching evaluation, I am reprimanded for allowing students too much time to engage with the concepts discussed in class and for not providing them answers to questions I might ask on a test.

———

Nishat comes over with her mom the second I am alone in the house and pulls me aside to ask, "Are you a *famous* writer?"

I don't know what to tell her. My picture has appeared on the cover of magazines printed in languages I can't read. Total strangers have proposed marriage, and others have submitted credible death threats. I've spent time in the company of people who inspired me to get into this business in the first place. People I've never met write me wonderful, heartfelt letters. A lot of letters. Once, a song. And I have managed to maintain any semblance of a career in a notoriously difficult-to-navigate field from which many of my contemporaries have justifiably fled. But I suspect what she is asking is whether or not I have been on TV, so I say, "It depends on what you mean by 'famous.'"

"Like, you write books"—she gazes at me, carefully considering her explanation—"and people read them?"

"Oh," I say, laughing. "Yes. If that is how we judge fame, then I am a famous writer."

Her eyes become round and sparkle, and I love her immediately. It is in fact the first time we meet. It is one thing for a writer to be excited about their own readers but quite another for a preteen girl to be impressed by their very existence. Reading! A quiet act with such profound implications!

Then, cementing our relationship, she asks, "Can *I* read them?"

————

The class of diseases I have are called autoimmune because they are the result of the body's immune system attacking its host, although little else is known about them, including why they start or how to stop them. It is known that a child born to parents with autoimmune diseases is more likely to develop their own autoimmune disease or diseases; it is even known which strains of disease in the parent tend to inspire which strains in their children. Physical trauma, such as exposure to certain toxins or sustained hunger, can also trigger an autoimmune response. They are strange diseases and cause an array of physical disabilities, some triggered by food sensitivities. However, they also offer interesting physical attributes: wounds heal unusually quickly and other illnesses can be easily eradicated. Women tend to get them more frequently than men, although funding for studies to examine causes and possible treatments are rare, facts that correlate neatly to women's diminished earning potential in a patriarchal society.

I write a book about these diseases, and gender, and our political economy. For several months I am offered relief from public conversations about my house and my lifestyle by having conversations instead about my ailments. It does not take very much time before I have exhausted my interest in answering personal questions.

———

I unpack my library enthusiastically, because I have never before had the opportunity for permanent book storage. Some boxes have been hidden under desks or on shelves for many years, and opening them is like introducing my oldest friends to new acquaintances I like very much. Other boxes have accumulated because I have recently written the books inside of them, or friends have, and I received them during a time of transition. And these are just the bound books: my zine collection will be saved for later unpacking. I take my time with the process and consider carefully how I will arrange the collection, because being a person who values books in Detroit now seems to be a significant part of my job.

I determine to turn the second bedroom into a library, maybe with a bed if it fits, but quickly fill the shelves I brought with me. I consider investing in new, locally constructed bookshelves and visit a furniture store, which doesn't have any bookshelves in stock. "Will you get more in?" I ask, since the salesperson seems to have noted the absence without interest.

"Probably not," she says.

Thinking I might have bookshelves made, I call a local woodworker, who says he has no expertise in this area. Even the used-furniture stores I visit have few bookshelf options, none satisfactory. I visit a new store that turns reclaimed materials into domestic furniture.

"Will you be making any bookshelves?" I ask the salesperson. "I can't imagine that we would," she answers honestly.

————

I decide to offer local colleges, universities, and high schools in the area fee-free speaking engagements in my first year in Detroit and contact several local schools and other programs about holding comics, writing, and zine-making workshops. Few have the infrastructure to manage guest speakers, however, and only one student group manages to book a date with me within that time period. After that I am too broke and must charge for my labor.

————

I am not a gardener before I move to Detroit, but my curiosity and isolation grow quickly and in equal measure, so I find I have both time and inclination to explore the process. I have read as well that microbes in soil may help ease the variety of gut bacterial deficiencies I harbor, and I quickly find this to be true. In fact, I soon discover that, if I wake with joint pain, it can be alleviated almost immediately by digging in the dirt, faster even than with the high-dose prescription pain relievers I keep on hand but fret over taking due to my already taxed liver. I become curious about composting and create a food-waste pile, and then another next to it, for a different kind of organic matter. I compost experimentally: vegetables, then meat scraps, then moving boxes, then tax forms. I collect manure from various sources and plant wildly: vegetables I have never heard of, fruits I cannot identify, even mushrooms. When I discover that my soil has a deficiency, I develop an organic system of supplements. When my basil becomes afflicted with fusarium wilt, I experiment with various means of eradicating the virus: solarizing the soil, cooking it in my oven. I begin eating what I grow, first as seasoning, then side dishes, soon entire meals, and eventually I can go for whole seasons without shopping at grocery stores. My body adapts. Certain damaging medications, I find, I can take less of, with no noticeable increase in pain. My blood pressure steadies, then drops. For entire months, it is almost as if I am not sick at all, a new person in a new body.

———

The exact amount of money Virginia Woolf called for in *A Room of One's Own* is five hundred British pounds per month, the rough 1928 equivalent of $2,530 today. This is significantly more than I make every month, and I—an unmarried cis woman with no children to raise—could live off it quite comfortably. Woolf's call for this particular monthly stipend offers a nice benchmark, a suggested starting place for grant-making bodies and significant donors to consider when establishing funding opportunities for women and perhaps nonbinary writers. In many ways, however, money and class and talent and professional opportunity are linked on a very deep level, especially when evaluating the work of women. I am well aware of the spaces my own work is denied entry for reasons that can be traced to my income level: I do not hold an MFA, I cannot afford certain prestigious residencies or workshops, and I occasionally miss out on speaking or reading opportunities for reasons of work or health. It is undeniably true that one can write without a minimum of $2,500 coming in every month, but I do wonder if one is everywhere considered a writer without a comfortable base of economic support and the literary opportunities such a sum allows for.

———

The restrictions on my ability to travel mean I must forgo several international speaking engagements and all journalistic assignments that require extended stays elsewhere. Consequently I go entirely without a paycheck for my first eight months in Detroit, and after that my earnings are significantly diminished since they are limited only to domestic, short-term projects. During this period I express concern to the organization that the experiment is not working, that if the organization is going to bring writers to Detroit they must be able to survive, and I urge the organization to allocate resources to expanding local opportunities for literary health, such as publishing or workshop programs. I notify the organization that I can no longer commit to the travel restrictions the program demands because I must be able to afford health insurance. I am able to eat, I realize, mostly because I have taken to growing my own food.

———

Although she stopped coming to class shortly after the midpoint in the semester, one of my students is upset by her grade. She fails to comprehend over email the impact her absences have on her standing, so I meet with her to explain in person. In this meeting, she apologizes for missing class, then tells me that she was diagnosed with a terminal disease, although she cannot offer the doctor's note required by the school to accept such an excuse. She insinuates that she is not expected to survive the summer. She asks for extra time on her final paper and the opportunity to rewrite it. I suggest that, if her time is indeed limited, she may wish to find more enjoyable activities to engage in. I have personally found it useful, I explain, as someone with several severe health issues myself—one of which, I do not mention, is the disease she has just described as terminal—to accept my limitations in the realm of work or academic performance and concentrate on doing what brings me joy. This, I suggest, can actually be quite healing. But she persists, explaining to me that her dying wish is to leave behind a B average. Additionally, the department chair steps in. The student rewrites the paper over the summer. When I see her again in the fall, her recovery is miraculous.

———

I buy a used pickup truck and become a person who stops suddenly near interesting piles of garbage. I load soil into the bed of my truck, or compost, and haul furniture for neighbors and friends. I antique shop in other time zones and buy gooseberry bushes on a whim, without pausing to question how to get them home. I am small, and it feels good to wield so many large items by myself. Powerful and fun, like when I eventually open a retirement account.

———

My main source of income and joy is the monthly comics journalism strip I do about Detroit with Melissa Mendes, a brilliant cartoonist, sharp editor, and empathetic collaborator based in Western Massachusetts. Our conversations are thoughtful and nuanced. Who I decide to interview and how I plan to shape each script is based on these conversations and her questions about the city. However, these discussions about the city stand in sharp contrast to my experience in the city. No one I am apt to see on any given day knows or perhaps cares what comics journalism is, so I must accept that one of my primary activities is wholly meaningless to most of the people I come across on a daily basis. However, this is true in other places I have lived. It is also true of other activities I engage in.

———

One of my students inserts a slide into their final presentation intended to point out that Henry David Thoreau looks a little bit like Ellen DeGeneres. The class devolves into laughter and appreciation of this point, and it is agreed by all to be significant. The student receives high marks in peer reviews of the presentation because of the trenchant observation. I, too, reward the student, for giving the only art history presentation that day to mention someone who is no longer alive.

———

I give away plant starts at the garden center, volunteering to hand out my favorite plant, brussels sprouts, to group members. I am fond of the plant because it looks silly, the leaves have a buttery taste when fried, and the sprouts are both adorably tiny and delicious with bacon, an important point none of my neighbors appreciate since they don't eat pork. Garden center members snake through long lines and stop at various stations to choose their plants, and I find I must make a pitch for brussels sprouts, which are not popular among new growers, and my station comes late in their line. My enthusiasm for the plant convinces many people to grow brussels sprouts, although not everyone. People who reject the plant make me a tiny bit sad, so I start saying, "Well, you don't *deserve* brussels sprouts," in a jokey voice when growers walk away without them.

Then someone retorts, "Hey, aren't you that person who writes books?" So I stop.

———

During my evening class one snowy day, my students begin packing their bags. "Uh," I say, because there are two more hours left in the class period and I am administering a midterm exam.

"We were told to go home," one says. She shows me her phone.

My students have all received text messages from the school's administration advising them that there is a snow emergency and that they should return home immediately.

"OK," I say. "Get home safe."

I receive no such notification from the school, via text, email, or otherwise. Not that day, nor the next. When I ask at the office why not, no one can tell me.

————

I show up at the lumberyard and say to the sweaty men covered in sawdust, "Can I have a bunch of your hardwood waste?" I tell them I can fit as much as they have in the bed of my truck.

"You must be one o' them mushroom punks," one drawls at me, although we are not in the South. It is true that I want to use the material as a mushroom substrate.

Later, I make myself a T-shirt: MUSHROOM PUNK. So there is no question.

————

In *The Culture Industry: Enlightenment as Mass Deception*, Theodore Adorno writes, "That the difference between the models of Chrysler and General Motors is fundamentally illusory is known by any child, who is fascinated by that very difference. The advantages and disadvantages debated by enthusiasts serve only to perpetuate the appearance of competition and choice." My students, whose parents design these cars, are agog at the statement in the reading I have assigned. They spend the class period arguing vehemently over the fundamental differences between Chrysler and General Motors, citing history, labor practices, and key design innovations. They do not believe these differences are illusory. Not by any stretch.

———

I begin hosting a reading series in my home to support the local writing community, but it is difficult to convince anyone to attend and, because I am immunocompromised, grows dangerous during cold and flu season. I find a local arts organization to host the series, but here people complain of having to drive to a different part of the city, and the cost of hosting the series doubles. Soon I have also run out of local writers willing to perform.

During this time, I make buttons that say, I READ AND I LIVE IN DETROIT. I make one hundred of them to give away to any Detroit residents who promise to wear them. After a year I still have thirty left.

———

An unwritten part of my contract with the organization stipulates that for the first two years I spend in the house, I will offer free, on-call, twenty-four-hour publicity and marketing support. That these rules are unwritten makes them difficult to discuss or negotiate, and often the public speaking I am asked to do comes at an inconvenient or difficult time. For example, I take a weekly medication that keeps me groggy, nauseous, and overemotional all day on Sundays, but this is the time the organization prefers to hold events, so I am often required to speak in public when I should be home vomiting. That I live without any real privacy for two years—a side effect of reporters asking endless questions about the layout of and activities within my home as well as of board members, potential donors, and tour groups stopping by often unannounced—also goes unacknowledged. At the time, I accept it, but when I later calculate my precise gains and losses in the free-house experience, I am surprised by how angry it makes me.

———

I discuss writing stories about the city with editors of various national journalistic outlets, but these editors are quick to point out that Detroit is "over" or that something was already written on the city, in another outlet, earlier in the year.

———

I am asked to teach a course on the history of American illustration and am given the syllabi of the previous courses taught in the department on the subject. They are all very similar, although they highlight different moments in the development of the field. However, all contain the same odd phrase in the course abstract: "A theoretical approach will be used to discuss the role of women in illustration." Indeed, there are no women listed on the syllabi at all, in any capacity. Not as researchers, historians, or illustrators.

―――――

My book about autoimmune disease and capitalism does well. Sells through the first printing quickly, is praised in the press and nominated for several awards, one national. A second printing is ordered, larger than the first, and this, too, sells out quickly. Then I stop hearing from my publisher. The book is gone. It is like a lost hard drive, or small arson. Several years of work vanished.

―――――

For the comics series, I meet Melissa Mays to discuss her central role in the Flint water crisis. We talk over coffee for several hours, because although I am there to interview her about her experiences, what we have in common is disease.

She's got light brown, almost blond hair now, although before the city of Flint famously switched its water source to the Flint River as a cost-saving measure on April 25, 2014, her hair was a dark brown. Only a few months after the switch, Mays's doctors suggested she may be autoimmune. Sudden food allergies, lupus-like symptoms, swollen joints, colon issues. No particular diseases have been diagnosed, because her symptoms are too plentiful. "I've got IBS and diverticulosis. Seizures. Lead and copper stored in my brain," she tells me. "I don't have MS and I don't have epilepsy, so hooray for that, but I have abnormalities in the back of my brain, which cause seizures and tremors. Also, my immune system is damaged to where my white blood cell count is little to nothing."

We discuss at length our shared frustration with medical professionals, who seem to understand little about a class of disease that is now becoming quite common. In her case, this frustration is compounded by the city's refusal, for far too long, to acknowledge that anything at all is wrong and its subsequent failure to own up to its role in it for even longer.

What I am struck by as we talk is how she trusted her local city government to provide basic services necessary for survival and was made sick by it. Of course, this is unjust, deplorable, and infuriating, but it has also caused permanent damage. Mays will never again be someone who was not poisoned by an entity entrusted to care for her and her family. That Flint, and Highland Park, and Detroit, and a growing number of cities throughout the state and region and country are made up of such individuals is staggering. The depth of rage. All justified.

I find myself in an uncomfortable situation: unable to process any further horrors on an emotional level but reliant on seeking them out for my job.

———

I speak to a group of teens in an art program. They are brilliant beyond their education level, as high schoolers often are: curious, enthusiastic, and eager to laugh. I tell them about traveling the world working with young women on self-publishing projects, and making journalism with comics when the only other people that do that in the world could all fit into a room together. High schoolers across the country at this time are walking out of class to show support for gun control legislation, and Detroit schools are threatening to expel anyone who participates. I tell them about being arrested for defending what I believe to be right, about being censored for making overtly political statements in art environments, about the loneliness of being the only girl in the room most of the time. They ask many questions throughout my talk, which I keep informal, so I can address their ideas, concerns, and questions as they arise. When I am done they have more questions. They pose them in this order:

"How do you do scary things without feeling fear?"

"Is it legal for them to expel us for walking out of school in protest?"

"Can you really show me how to make my own magazine or was that a joke?"

————

After one lecture on the history of industrial design, a jury of my students finds me guilty of "slagging off on Eli Whitney too harsh."

"Wait until capitalism starts to fail you," I tell them. "Then we'll see who has slagged off too harsh upon whom." I don't necessarily know what it means, but the more ridiculously I protest, the more likely they are to remember the name Eli Whitney in the future.

Publishers Weekly writes enthusiastically of my next book and I spend days trying to track down anyone who has heard of *Publishers Weekly* so I can share my excitement in person. I fail.

After teaching for two years in Detroit, a former student, no longer in any of my classes, tells me she checked out my book from interlibrary loan. She expresses dismay that the school I teach at does not carry my books, although they are used as texts in schools elsewhere. "It was really good!" she says, eyes wide. "I can't believe you teach here!"

But by this time I have already submitted my notice.

6

THE NEIGHBORS

I tried to remember any case in the course of my reading where two women are represented as friends.

—VIRGINIA WOOLF, *A Room of One's Own*

The six-year-old across the street grows concerned that I do not know enough about the color red and enrolls me immediately in something she calls "red school," which she happens to teach. From then on, whenever she spots me in my garden, she comes to her porch to deliver a lengthy monologue inspired by the color red. "Red is the color of roses," she may begin and then list other things that are also red. Often she will name the various emotions associated with red, including anger or love. Sometimes, she forgets that she is talking about anything in particular at all and just says words for a while, sometimes including the word "red," but not always. Where red school becomes really interesting is when she begins slipping the color into phrases she has heard elsewhere but perhaps not fully understood. "If you give your love to red, it will give it right back to you," she tells me once.

———

For months, there is talk of Sadia's brother's impending marriage and all of the various outfits involved. It is an exciting time. Plans are made, websites consulted, traditions explained to me, the outsider who is expected to participate. Then suddenly the plans are scrapped and I am invited to a party and asked to bring my Christmas tree lights and all the flowers I can part with from my front garden.

"Emergency wedding," Sadia says very solemnly.

———

For several weeks after I first move in, video from the local news broadcast of my first day in the house is passed around the local high schools by Nishat and Sadia. They also pore over my social media accounts and comment on them frequently to each other in my presence. For a time, I am what marks them as cool, notable among their peers. Then I am a resource, someone with inside knowledge about matters conducted in English: the language itself, laws, bureaucracy, subjects studied in school. Eventually I become just a neighbor, which is better.

———

Funny story. On November 8, 2016, I join the rest of my neighborhood at our local polling place to cast our votes for the next president of the United States of America. The signage at my polling place is in Arabic and Bangla. Most of the other voters are women, presumably because it is in the middle of the day and their husbands are working. There are only a handful of voters present without head scarves. I am the only white woman in the room.

"So," a woman to my left says as we wait for a booth to open. She is Black, with creamy, dark skin, sparkling eyes, and a wide, quick grin. "Where's the Hillary victory party?"

A younger woman wearing a head scarf titters nearby. An older Bengali woman to my right says solemnly, "I will cook." She nods her head slightly. Others voice interest.

"OK," the first woman says. "But where *the party* at?"

A young woman who works at a local restaurant suggests the banquet hall of her employer. Dishes are allocated. Someone offers to chip in for beverages. A time is designated; a voice wonders if televisions can be located and brought in so we can watch the results on cable. Very quickly the entire gymnasium is filled with excitable, high voices, eagerly planning our future. Immediately, we vote. That night, we celebrate. Tomorrow, we will live in a world where someone like us—a woman in the United States— becomes one of the most powerful people in the world.

It is true and sad enough that the party never happens. More upsetting is that voting machines across Detroit malfunction that day, and according to a December 18, 2016, *Free Press* report, at over 248 precincts in the city, more votes are tallied than voters had requested ballots. Policies dictate that, because there is no clear manner of establishing true from improper or duplicate votes, the votes in these precincts—ours included—must be discarded. In this way, when Donald Trump becomes president of the United States, the women in my neighborhood cannot say they voted against him. Their votes against him did not even count.

———

The morning the Parkland students are first in the news, agitating for gun control legislation and an immediate end to school shootings, Sadia comes running up to me after school yelling, "ANNE DID YOU HEAR WHAT THE TEENAGERS IN FLORIDA ARE DOING?"

"Yes. I'm right here," I tell her. "You don't have to ye—"

"HOW DO WE DO THAT," she demands, cutting me off.

———

I order some extra trees from a nursery to plant around the neighborhood with the girls. We spend a day choosing locations and asking permission and digging holes and planting pink- and white-flowering trees in spots that used to be dumping grounds, burned-down houses, piles of crumbling concrete. I charge the girls with making sure the saplings are watered every day and teach them how to make sure the growing plants get enough moisture. Within a week each tree, in each separate location, has died. They are mowed down by lawn mowers, trodden on by men, or crushed by forgotten building supplies.

———

The invitation to my very first iftar, the meal eaten in the evenings during Ramadan, is super casual. "Just come over, 8:51, 8:52," my neighbor says, waving her hand nonchalantly.

———

I walk across the street one day in the middle of summer with no shoes on and chat with the children a bit. "Anne," they say, "you forgot your shoes!"

"Oh, no," I scoff. "It's No-Shoe Tuesday. Where I come from, you don't wear shoes on Tuesday."

For three years, every Tuesday, the girls across the street scream "No-Shoe Tuesday!" at me and fling their footwear across the porch, no matter the season.

———

Shortly after the 2017 presidential inauguration, I attend a neighborhood meeting. A Muslim woman I don't know turns to me and asks, "Can you tell me what happens when people get arrested? I need to know what I'm in for."

———

The summer I am twenty-eight, Thurber and I live in my pickup truck and travel the country. We move to Seattle together, and also Boston, then back to Chicago. Of all the places he has lived, he is most comfortable in Detroit, where I can leave the clear plastic-screened front door closed but he can still see all the neighbors from the floor, stare attentively at their doings, and meow if he sees any suspicious activity. He is a fixture; the neighbors greet him as they walk by, by name, even neighbors I have not met. He is more popular than I am.

———

I ask a neighbor boy what he's up to one afternoon. "Just waitin' for puberty," he responds. Then I don't see him for a while.

A year and a half later, he is suddenly a man.

———

I go to the home and garden center with a generous friend who wants to support my new life endeavor by purchasing supplies and appliances. We take a big grocery cart through the store and race down relevant aisles—paint, shelving, storage—barely consulting each other as we lob in ridiculous home goods. In the garden aisles, my friend goes whole hog: hoes, rakes, electric branch trimmers. I stop him at the elaborate nozzle he has chosen for my garden hose. He believes he has selected a state-of-the-art tool that I will use every day. But what I see is a shiny, overly elaborate gewgaw that my neighbors will see me using daily, a tool far fancier than I would ever need.

"That's a nozzle for rich people," I tell him sternly as I replace it on the shelf.

———

Whenever something inexplicable occurs in relation to my house, or anyone's house, I explain to the girls in serious tones about housetubes, the nonplumbing tubes that exist inside a home that are essential to its function but that you are not supposed to talk about. Soon the fiction becomes common parlance, used to explain away unusual noises, crumbling walls, water damage, and mysterious repairs the neighbors undertake. "It must be the housetubes," Sadia whispers to me one day when three men down the block unpack a ladder from their truck.

————

The neighbor girls don't entirely understand how I came to be living in this house, possibly because they don't understand home ownership, a complicated notion anyway, made more confusing here by the two-year rent-free residency agreement. They may also find my situation confusing because, for the younger girls, the very concept of time is shaky. The six-year-old across the street, for example, does not understand that before I lived in this house, I lived somewhere else. However, they do understand the concept of winning a free house, because that's normal to them now, since they see someone that happened to every day. Once, when we walk by a moving van on our Evening Constitutional, one of the girls wonders aloud whether the couple seated inside just won that house.

One spring day I clarify that, in a few months, it will be two years that I have lived in the house, and that will be when I finally, legally own it. I add that if, before that time, they decide they don't like me, or I suddenly go crazy and decide I don't like them, we can just tell the organization and they will make me move and give the house to someone else.

At first, the girls are appalled. "Why would we do that? We would never do that! What a terrible idea!" Sadia and the six-year-old across the street agree. Then they think about it more, and a series of questions begins. If I had to move away, would I take my cat or would he still live in the house without me or, better yet, need to move in with one of them? Would the new person who moved in maybe be more interesting than I am? If I had to move away would I stay on this block?

"Well, no," I reply to this last. "If I had to move out because you guys decided you didn't like me, I think I would at least move to a different block." But what if they had me kicked out so that even more interesting people could come live on our block and then they just built me another house next door to my current neighbors, on the other side, just two lots down? This is the plan they eventually agree to.

———

One early fall afternoon, an unidentified chicken is wandering around the front yards of the houses across the street. No one on this part of the block raises chickens, so I watch it with interest for a few minutes. Eventually it enters the house directly across the street. Although three excitable children under the age of seven live there, there is no ensuing commotion. In fact, no one seems to care. No further notice of the event is taken. Life proceeds as normal.

———

Many of my neighbors refer to me as American, to distinguish from themselves as Bengali. Sometimes, however, they are not referring to national heritage but race. When they ask if Americans will be at a certain event, they often mean white people.

———

I invite the neighbor girls over to help me plant squash, because activities that retain the appearance of helpfulness but are actually just excuses to talk seem to be their favorites, and I do not need help planting squash. They arrive in their typical flowing attire. After Sadia's head scarf falls in her eyes too many times, she dramatically removes it and places it to rest on a nearby trellis. I have refrained until this moment from asking about their head scarves, or when they do or do not wear them, but I pose the question to Sadia now. "Oh, if it's just us girls, it doesn't matter," she says. I still have questions, but I am so flattered to be included in the intimacy that I save them for later.

———

The six-year-old across the street suggests that I grow my hair long. "Like it is on Google," she adds.

———

When I have white friends over to my house, my neighbors come to the porch to meet them, fawning over them enthusiastically. The youngest children happily translate all questions from their parents, play with women's long hair, and giggle. When I have Southeast Asian friends over to my house, my neighbors are flabbergasted. They ask where they were born, what foods they ate growing up, where their families are. After these friends leave, my neighbors demand further details at every chance, ask when these friends will return, inquire after their whereabouts and mothers. When I have Black friends over, the young children are silent, uncomfortable. The elders in the neighborhood still ask questions, but no one will translate them.

———

Nishat's mom brings Thurber some curried chicken, and thereafter, when he smells curry wafting from her stove, he meows out the window toward her kitchen next door, running to me if I move or change positions or even glance up from my desk, attempting to herd me toward the smell. All Girl Metal Band does not care for Bengali cuisine. She doesn't like people food at all, or unusual cat foods. She doesn't even like treats or catnip. She likes dry cat food from a bag, served in a bowl and placed on the floor.

———

Occasionally people unfamiliar with Detroit ask if I feel safe in my neighborhood and I burst out laughing because I've never felt more safe. In truth I am overly protected, sometimes coddled, and most of the time way closer to bored.

———

One day my curiosity about head scarves is finally satiated. It turns out Nishat and Sadia like them because they provide an extra piece of fashion to play with every day. Sadia says it also protects her hair from getting too hot in the sun but admits she mostly wears the hijab for style reasons.

"Did you start wearing them because your moms do?" I ask, wondering how much familial pressure comes into their fashion decisions.

"Actually my mom didn't wear one," Nishat says. She first put one on one day when she brought her daughter to preschool, hoping to signal her identification with other Bengali parents.

"I saw it and liked it and wanted to wear one, too," Nishat says. So from then on, they both wore head scarves, she and her mom.

———

One particular neighbor comes into my garden fairly regularly, an elderly woman who does not speak to me. I do not mind until the day she takes offense at my herb garden and begins plucking mint and thyme out of their containers by the roots. Other times, she just wanders by to take some vegetables.

———

At night, Nishat and Sadia gather on the front steps to speak in hushed tones about people who appear in YouTube videos. They call them YouTubers, and one night I decide to ask them what all the fuss is about. They spend an hour detailing the intricate goings-on of people they have never met, describe what these people like and dislike, what they wear, what they eat, what they think is funny, people whose lives seem to take place primarily in their own bedrooms or backyards. These are people who decide they want to be famous by making self-confessional videos and then become famous for making self-confessional videos, each decision inconceivable to me, repellent. I hear about YouTubers' friends, families, antics, and then there is still more. But I can discern nothing at all about these people with money, usually white people, usually young men, that is interesting to me or that I can mine to help these girls understand something about the world or themselves. "I will not talk about YouTubers anymore," I say when the hour is up, "until you start your own YouTube channel." They are too shy at first, but a couple years later, Nishat becomes a minor Instagram sensation.

———

For her birthday, I give Nishat a comic book, *Lumberjanes*, popular among young women for its strong female characters and quality of writing. She and Sadia read it immediately and like it a lot. Then they tell me they have discussed which of the characters my friends and I most closely resemble, based on sense of humor, adventurousness, love of books, and hair color. They list these characters, pairing them with only my white friends, possibly because the characters in the book I have given them are all white-passing. They do not name themselves. I ask them more about what they like about the book, and what they think it is about. Normal girls, they say. Americans. It becomes clear that they do not see themselves reflected in it in any way.

———

I eventually grow to love how Detroiters ask, "Where do you live?" and expect me to respond with a street address, as if they've never gotten a death threat. However, it does take a while.

———

Nishat's mom pronounces "sleeping" and "slipping" virtually the same, and doesn't use the past tense, so when she explains why I shouldn't use the icy walkway between our two houses anymore—because she is sleeping—you can understand why I would be confused.

———

One of the odder aspects of my agreement with the organization is that I maintain an alarm system as well as a sign in front of the house clearly displaying the brand of alarm. I have lived in areas of extreme poverty before, where such signs are deliberately removed so that burglars are not alerted to the fact that you have valuables you wish to keep from being stolen. I am also annoyed by the fact that my alarm system appears to be broken even upon installation and goes off at random moments for no reason, which sends the whole neighborhood into a slight panic. Is my house being broken into? Will theirs be next? What I come to understand, however, is that the signs are common around the city, but the alarms they supposedly signify are significantly less so. That I both have a sign indicating an alarm and an alarm that can occasionally be heard throughout the neighborhood comes to be seen as an indication that our neighborhood is the kind of neighborhood with alarm systems, not to be fucked with.

———

By chance while traveling I stumble across the U.S. premiere of the Italian film *Bangla*, about a young man growing up in an Italo-Bengali community in Rome who falls in love with an Italian girl, throwing his family into mild panic. The film is warm and funny and feels familiar to me, although it does not in any way address the needs or interests of young Bengali women. I ask the filmmaker, present, what he might say to my neighbor girls back home who may soon find themselves struggling with some of the same questions his film raises—about marriage and sex and cultural preservation—but from the perspective of young women.

"Good luck" is all the advice he offers, his eyes wide.

———

A neighbor and I develop a network of gossip across our front porches during the warm months. At first, she spends much time informing me of the details of local crimes: shootings, arsons, theft. There is an abandoned house the next block over, and meth users squat there, cutting through her yard to walk down our street to their next destination. Most of these meth users are white and pass by unremarked upon. But the two or three Black folks who frequent the house are the subject of much conversation.

———

There is an opossum in the neighborhood, and he seems to favor my garden, which I do not mind because opossums are good pest control and because the neighbor who hates mint believes it to be a large rat.

———

Nishat's mom and I drive past my favorite abandoned factory on Ryan Road while running an errand. "I love that place," I tell her. It's got an art deco façade but the building is filled with abandoned tires and trees that grow through former floorboards. "I want to buy it someday and start up the production line!"

"Anne. What would you do with this factory," she says. She does not pose it as a question, with an inflection at the end of the sentence, but as a statement. Her brother is in government and she has been raised to demand information, not inquire after it.

"Obviously cats," I say. Like this is a legitimate business.

"It a good idea," she agrees. Then there is a pause. Our relationship has developed quickly over the last year, and she no longer asks if I am serious when I say ridiculous things. Presumably, she has seen me do enough ridiculous things that she is aware that I am always mostly serious.

After another moment passes she says, "Anne. You buy this factory, for cats, and all the Bengali women work there."

For several months I try to figure out what my Bengali Cat Factory could do, but I am unable to secure start-up funds.

————

The teenaged boys in my neighborhood are all exceedingly polite, and even when they get together at night to cause trouble or do some marauding, they usually end up staying within earshot of their mothers or fixing another neighbor's car for free. I keep hoping that I will catch them at the neighborhood skate park, but none of them ever go there, I suspect because they are shy in front of other kids. Finally, one day, I get very excited about the possibility that there are some real troublemakers around when I spot some spray-painted text on the side of first one building, then another. The same text. It is nearly illegible in both occurrences, but the word "Rupna" can be read clearly. I ask around about who the vandal is, the tagger, but no one knows. Finally I meet a young girl who has information on the hoodlum. "It's my brother Rupna," she says. "It means 'Rupna is the best.'"

"Ah!" I say. "And he is tagging the neighborhood!" I am thrilled.

"No," she says, "first just our house. He had to wait a few

weeks before he got permission to write it also on our grandma's house."

———

When a particularly suspicious person is spotted in the neighborhood, I will occasionally receive a knock on my door. At first I take this seriously and resolve to keep an eye out after every interruption. But then I notice that the concern always hinges around the same thing, the utterance at my door always some variation on the statement "Anne, did you see? A Black man!"

———

The massive empty lot on the corner across the street from my house is used as a dumping ground because it was never a house, only an empty space next to a vacant commercial space, no family to be mourned. Miraculous objects sometimes appear there when you need them, including spare wood or free tires or old apple crates. Once I find a rusty metal cabinet, formerly white but oxidized to a pleasing cream with orange-brown spots, designed to hold tools. Very early one morning I carry it back to my house. I intend to use it to hold my clothes although it only has one door. I hose it down, then clean it more thoroughly before bringing it inside. When I step outside again, Nishat's mom is digging through the pile of rotting, abandoned pallets and bags of garbage to locate the door, which she dutifully carries toward me and hands over, without saying a word.

———

The rules regarding parking are obscure. To park directly in front of someone else's house is a sign of disrespect, and I am often asked to move my car if it is situated too close to a neighbor's yard. Parking in front of my house seems to be OK, though, for everyone, and it is unclear why. Often the same person parks in front of my house while visiting a neighbor, his relative, and his van is massive, larger than most vans. Unsurprisingly, he is an aggressive, large man who speaks mostly to other men and yells at his children. When I ask him to move his van, he laughs and begins a conversation with the nearest man.

When I later float the notion among my neighbors of selling my house, however, he begins speaking to me. He demands that I sell him my house for approximately half its market value. "Cash!" he screams from the middle of the street, even though all the houses in this neighborhood sell for cash. I tell him that I will not sell him my house. He undertakes then an aggressive campaign of parking in front of my yard, leaving his van there for days at a time, even when he goes elsewhere. However, this fails to intimidate me into selling him my house.

———

At a small-craft fair, I see an acquaintance in comics who has recently moved to Detroit. She runs a distribution house for books by women of Arabic descent, and her titles are displayed on the table. Although most have adult themes, one is by a Bengali artist, and I cannot pass up the chance to give it to Sadia, a late birthday present. It is a queer coloring book, so too young for her, on one hand, as she no longer colors, and too old for her, on the other, because it contains explicit, queer imagery that could upset a parent. Driving home to deliver the gift, I consider offering her a content warning or suggesting she keep the book at my house, but by the time I have decided I should definitely say *something*, she has taken the book onto the steps to pore over its full-page, black-and-white illustrations. She reads the Arabic to me, then translates it. She asks me what pinkwashing is, and drag. She stops at the image of a young woman with text describing her as dark skinned but still beautiful. "That happens," Sadia says, her eyes wide with recognition. "No one in Bangladesh thinks dark-skinned girls like me can be beautiful."

———

Eventually one neighbor pulls me aside. "Anne. Why so many Black people at your house?"

"They are my friends," I say. And "This is Detroit." I say, "You do not get to tell me who is allowed at my house and who is not." I also say, "I do not think we should judge people on the color of their skin." I ask the neighbor if she has ever felt like she was being judged on the color of her skin but receive no answer. In fact, it's a good question: Can a Muslim woman in America ever feel as if race were the sole implicating factor in any discomfort she may feel? I do not know.

I also do not know whether the exchange has caused her to reconsider her feelings about Black people in the neighborhood. Only that she no longer expresses those feelings to me. I have no idea if this is an improvement or not.

———

The neighbors discover that a daughter, still in Bangladesh, will have a child and come live with them in Detroit, so they plan a celebrational feast. The father borrows a motorcycle and returns a few hours later with a live chicken tied to the back, which escapes the moment he unties it. After recapturing the chicken, he picks it up by its neck, poses for my picture, and brings it into his backyard to slaughter, which I also photograph. I am delighted by the excitement, although I can only communicate this visually, by jumping up and down and smiling openly. The elder members of this family do not speak any English, and the daughter who does is still in school. When the excitement dies down, I return to work, eat dinner, and go to bed.

After midnight there is a loud and terrifying pounding on my bedroom window. When I open the door, the school-age daughter yells, "Come, come!" I slip on some clothes and accompany her across the street. I fear a horrible danger has befallen the family and I am being summoned to describe it for the police. Instead I find that the curry has finished cooking and I am being offered a bowl.

———

I am loading boxes into the back of my pickup truck when I notice a young man seated inside his car parked a few yards away, facing me but engrossed in his cell phone. Another young man across the street eyes him suspiciously from his front porch. This young man usually spends his days fixing cars with the other young Bengali men in the neighborhood, and on the Fourth of July is in charge of the block's unofficial fireworks, which always begin at sundown and end by eleven o'clock, so everyone can get to bed at a reasonable hour. My neighbor approaches me, asking at first if I need any help. When he is near enough to me, he says seriously, "What do you think of the man in that car?"

I had not thought much about him, only noticed him, but it is true that the man is Black. I become concerned because so many of my neighbors have openly expressed worry about Black people in the neighborhood that I fear they will attempt to engage him in a negative way. As my mind works through the mechanics of my concern, I realize that there is very little difference between this and being concerned that there is a Black man in the neighborhood.

"He's fine," I say.

"I don't know," my neighbor says.

"I'll go talk to him." I feel I am being forced to perform a racist act in order to stave off an even more racist act later. Is it better if I mediate this or let it play out? Is it better if I hurt people or let them hurt one another and not participate? I do not know.

"Hey, man," I say to the kid, who is sitting in his car. I can now see what he is looking at on his phone. It is porn.

"Hey," he says.

"You need anything?" I ask. "You've been sitting out here for a while."

"I'm waiting for my friend," he says. He gestures toward the house he is parked in front of.

The house he is parked in front of is where the man lives who borrowed a cup of water to wash his sick wife's hair. This neighbor's English is limited and his interest in non-Bengali people is in question. I doubt that they are friends but do not perceive my role in this exchange to be one of judgment. I have been seen by my neighbors talking to this young Black man and I hope it eases tension.

"Cool," I say. "If you need anything, let me know."

To the young man across the street, I say, "He's fine." My neighbor still looks agitated, but it is unclear what form his nervousness may take. He is not a violent person by nature.

Later that night, nothing happens.

———

Bengali writer Taslima Nasrin names her 1998 book *Meyebela*, a word she coined, she says, because no other exists in Bangla to describe the state known in English as girlhood.

———

When the cat the neighbor girls call Metal Van dies, it is winter, so I store her body in a cardboard box in my freezer. As soon as possible in the spring, the girls decide to hold a funeral, citing three reasons: one, they have never been to a cat funeral; two, they have developed a theory that if we do not bury her soon, she will come back to life and feel cold in my freezer; and three, that her cold, lifeless body is taking up space where I would normally store Popsicles. So early one spring day, a few friends come by, along with all the girls in the neighborhood. Wracked by grief and guilt, I dig a deep hole and place my little cat's cold body with her unbelievably soft fur and one cat toy, safe in her cardboard coffin, at the bottom of the hole. Everyone present says something nice that they remember about her. I fill the hole with soil. We spend the rest of the day eating Popsicles and writing a space opera.

———

Nishat's mom has been waiting several years for an appointment to take her citizenship exam and finally receives one for the middle of December. Although she has lived in this country for nearly two decades, she studies for the test diligently, occasionally bringing up study points in casual conversation. Unfortunately I cannot converse for very long about Woodrow Wilson, and it becomes immediately apparent that the citizenship test demands far more information than is ever needed to be a citizen of the United States.

She takes her test while I wait in the lobby, surrounded by families and friends of test takers speaking naturally in dozens of languages. Across the street is a billboard for a lawyer offering immigration assistance, and soon, the lawyer himself appears in the lobby, comforting one family member and congratulating another.

My neighbor passes her exam easily, coming out from the exam room beaming at me shyly from under her seafoam-green-and-yellow head scarf. "My good luck," she says to the woman seated across from me, a blond Ukrainian still awaiting her appointment. My neighbor indicates me with a nod of her head and squeezes my shoulders.

————

Fariha, up the street, will not look at me if her parents are nearby, and her parents do not acknowledge me at all, so when she visits me one day I understand that she has undertaken the act illicitly. Obviously Fariha is not her real name. On the off chance that her parents learn to read English and decide to read this book, I will not endanger her by using her real name and describing her defiance of her parents' wishes. Still, she visits me in my home once, while her brothers play protectively in my yard, and is delighted that I own so many books. "Like a library!" she says in wonder and begins reading one right away. She comes again a few days later to, as she says, "see another book."

"I can teach you how to make one of those," I say casually, something I say to all young people excited about books everywhere, but have said to so many young Bengali women at this point to no avail that I am convinced it will go nowhere.

"When?" she says.

"When you come back. Tomorrow, if you like, or the next day." I know she will not return, that we can make very concrete plans and I can buy special materials and show them to her on the way home from the store but also that she will never actually sit down with me to learn how to make her own books.

For two and a half years I have put every imaginable effort into convincing the young women of Detroit, in this neighborhood and elsewhere, not only to love and value literature but to wield it as a tool. This is the week I am giving up, packing all my belongings to take a new job in a different city, convinced that the disregard for literacy in the schools and bookshelves in the furniture stores and books in the libraries all point to a basic truth about the way writing is valued here. It is not. And it is no great leap to surmise that my estimation of writing is equally unwelcome.

Fariha does not come the next day. But she does come the day after that and asks me to show her how to make a zine. And I do. It is amazing.

––––––

My neighbor's citizenship ceremony is set for the Monday before Donald Trump's inauguration. My status as "good luck charm" has earned me an invitation, and I anticipate it eagerly, although I do not know what to expect.

The judge opens with a historical overview, pulling few punches in acknowledging the history of violence, land seizure, genocide, slavery, and greed on which the country is founded. She does not mention "opportunity" once. Her welcome remarks are bold, vituperative: she describes this moment of new citizenship as the onset of a fight. As she elaborates on her theme, she moves toward an advocacy of responsibility, defined very narrowly: becoming a citizen of the United States now, she suggests, includes the responsibility to support current and future citizens of the United States. She speaks eloquently of Barack Obama's inauguration, inspirationally, even, and her silence on the pending inauguration speaks volumes.

Then, at the moment when other judges would perhaps offer a heartfelt welcome to their new, legal homeland, she instead issues a warning: "There will be some who do not believe you have your documents in order. Get your documents in order," she says sternly.

Then, forty-eight people from Iraq, Bangladesh, Yemen, India, Syria, Pakistan, Egypt, and Mexico are declared Americans. It is one of the most exciting events I have ever witnessed. The joy! The relief!

Two weeks later, new immigration restrictions are put in place by executive order. I calculate what might have happened if the citizenship ceremony I witnessed had been delayed. Then I would have witnessed the induction of only eighteen new American citizens.

7

THE COMMUNITY

I am by no means confining you to fiction. If you
would please me—and there are thousands like me—
you would write books of travel and adventure, and
research and scholarship, and history and biography,
and criticism and philosophy and science. By doing so
you will certainly profit the art of fiction. For books
have a way of influencing each other.

—VIRGINIA WOOLF, *A Room of One's Own*

While on a stroll together, two elderly women stop by to inform me that there are two kinds of parsley: tasty, delicious parsley from their home country and the kind that I am growing. Then they move on.

———

I locate the pickup truck that I want, a 2007 Ford Ranger 4x4, and go to the suburban used car lot to purchase it. I am in a rush; I have been renting a car from a staff member of the organization a few days per week, but she has decided to sell it suddenly, a few days before I have a book event several hours north. Also I cannot do without a car in Detroit for longer than a week, given the distance to grocery stores and pharmacies.

It is not my first Ranger; the turning radius is impressive and the engines generally solid. However, after driving a few miles away from the lot, the check engine light comes on. I am so distracted by it, and consumed with the fear that I have made a terrible mistake, that I do not hear the entire exhaust system creak off rustily and hit the ground.

I find the nearest mechanic, who asks me if I want to replace the exhaust system or just leave it. "Uh, replace it?" I say. "I think . . . it's the law?"

"Not in Michigan," he says. Then adds, "It's cheaper if you don't."

I replace the exhaust system.

———

Before I move to Detroit, my doctor cannot figure out what is wrong with me and takes me off all my medications at the same time. Within a week I am confined to bed, pain emanating from every part of my body. My right wrist is particularly aggravated: it becomes so inflamed that it ruptures the tendon, and I am forced to go to the emergency room, finally unable to withstand this stinging pain on top of the bed of sharp ache I am already experiencing. Soon I am remedicated and, within weeks, able to move freely again in all parts of my body except my right wrist. I wear a brace for several months, try to write with my left hand, and baby the joint. Packing and moving are difficult, although my friends help. Once I am resettled in the house, however, it is impossible to unpack boxes or work in the yard without using the wrist. I grow accustomed to a certain volume of daily pain, and take what drugs I can to ease it, but resign myself to persistent annoyance. When I begin eradicating stumps, however, my wrist once again becomes so inflamed that I cannot use my arm at night. I can't type. I must lie on my back without moving any part of my body below the shoulder, a position in which I have trouble sleeping.

The State of Michigan, during this time, cancels my health insurance for unclear reasons. Without oversight or medicine, the likelihood that I will require emergency care increases drastically, but I cannot find a way to explain to my neighbors that I am sick or what kinds of care I may need. When I initiate conversations about invisible disabilities, or food-related ailments, or my struggling liver, they see only a white woman with all her limbs who was given a house.

———

Nishat's mother's mother, still in Bangladesh, gets sick during the time that our Yemeni and Syrian neighbors are being stopped at the border. There is fear that if her mother's condition worsens, and she leaves the country to visit before taking her citizenship test, Nishat's mother may be unable to return. She spends weeks fretting. Then her mother dies. Nishat's mother is devastated.

A ceremony is held, to which I am invited. I had been to neighbors' homes before, for all-purpose celebrations—barbecues, New Year's Day festivities, birthday parties—and to a handful of more intimate family gatherings, but only after the prayers have ended. It is particularly important to my neighbor that I am there for the prayer ceremony. So I knock on the front door at the appropriate time. Inside, I can see the front room crowded with men in conversation. When a young man opens the door, he shoos me toward the rear of the house, the back door. The women's entrance.

———

There is much talk in Chicago of the meaning of community, and through these conversations I come to find my own communities through shared interests in art, books, social justice, and research. When I go to Cambodia, I develop a different understanding of community, one more like family, where a group of people form a consistent presence in a life that is not primarily social but both corrective and encouraging. There I am forced to rely on very young women from the provinces for cues to getting along in the foreign city; they suffer my questions and ignorance with grace, and from them I learn something about reliability and a great deal about love. While there, I maintain my community in Chicago, a distant but supportive presence that wants the best for me and for the people I come to love, whom they, too, come to love. But in Detroit, I am adrift. Local acquaintances fail to evolve into friendships; the strong focus on building traditional nuclear families seems to curtail a larger sense of community sustainability. Too, the side-gig hustle lends many interactions the frisson of commercial exchange. I find transactional relationships difficult to build community around.

———

It's a quiet night so I decide to introduce the neighbor girls to the concept of Ted Cruz being the Zodiac Killer, a theory they consider with growing interest, soon whipping out cell phones to Google the more complicated parts of the easily disprovable story. When I have completed my argument that the former candidate for U.S. president, born in 1970, probably killed several people in the late 1960s, their questions, in order, are:

"Who is Ted Cruz?"

"What is a zodiac?"

"Why is a presidential candidate murdering people?"

"Why does *The New York Times* think this is a joke?"

———

I technically live in Detroit, four blocks north of Hamtramck, the city with the first majority-Muslim city council, which famously installed public speakers to blast the call to prayer five times daily. My neighbors all have speakers installed inside their homes, too, and so five times per day, I am reminded with beautiful song that thousands of people around me want peace in the world and right at that very second are asking God for it in ways I do not comprehend. Under a story that mentions my residency in the area, an internet commenter asks how I like living under "Sharia Law."

———

Although people tell me they request it, the general-purpose literary bookstore in town will not stock my work. The bookstore in Ann Arbor carries it, but forty-five minutes is a long drive for folks who are only passingly curious about the new girl in town.

———

I am invited to a women-only spiritual cleanse, and there is little to do that weekend so, although spiritual cleanses are not really my thing, I go. Detroit's renowned hustle is strong that night, and several aspects of the spiritual cleanse include sales pitches for online aura readings and crystals and individual cleansing sessions. I follow through on none of them and that night feel significantly dirtier, spiritually speaking, than I had before the cleanse.

———

The vet pets my cat during a visit and then touches her mouth briefly. For the rest of our twenty-minute visit, she tries in vain to remove cat hair from her tongue. She is the best vet I have ever had.

———

Easily the most gutting architectural experience of my life is stumbling across the charred, crumbling beams of a house on the northwest side. A friend and I get out of the car and explore, expressing wonder and guilt and fascination in equal measure. The roof is gone, only a few corners of building still standing, and full daylight shines on a space intended to remain interior, protected, safe. It is discomforting. We read the daily lives of the former inhabitants, even now, like tea leaves. The contents of the burned half structure have been picked through, with only functionless children's toys—plastic princess tricycles melted beyond usability, model horses with singed manes and distended limbs—sacrificed to the land. Undisturbed is a whole children's library, remarkably undamaged, that no one thinks to plunder.

———

While my comics collaborator Melissa is in town, we ask the neighbor girls' parents for permission to interview their daughters for our project over mishti at Aladdin, the local Bengali restaurant and sweetshop. Surprisingly, all the parents agree, including the mother of the six-year-old across the street, so she and her younger sister, Nishat, Sadia, Melissa, and I all take the mile-long trek together, my cell phone set to record our conversation.

En route, I ask if they remember meeting one another, and they all scream excitedly except for the youngest girl, who remains entirely silent the whole time we record, a rare state for her.

"I met Nishat when I was a baby," the six-year-old says, but Sadia explains that their histories are more intertwined than that. Sadia's mother knew Nishat's mother from the masjid; Sadia's father taught Nishat's brother before Sadia had even arrived from Bangladesh. Everyone except Sadia lived in different houses in the neighborhood before settling into their present locales, where, by dint of proximity, they grew inseparable. "My parents know her parents very well," Sadia says. "They might be best friends."

Sadia's family moved relatively recently. "My dad, he came with three of my brothers and my sister first. I was around six, seven years old. Then my mom and us younger siblings came a few years after my dad and the older siblings. They wouldn't give us the visa all at once," she clarifies.

"So when you guys met—" I begin, and Sadia jumps in.

"I was thirteen," she says.

"But that was just before I came," I say, sure she must have gotten her dates mixed up.

"Yeah. I came to this house just before you came," Sadia says, and I am surprised at the rapidity with which her friendship with Nishat cohered.

Nishat's father has told me he has lived in the neighborhood for thirty-five years, which makes him one of the earliest Bengali residents of what is now called Banglatown. "He left Bangladesh when he was fourteen, fifteen?" Nishat says. He moved around for a while after that. I know he was in Germany and Austria for some time, then New York.

"But how long until your mom came?" I ask Nishat.

"They met each other in New York," she says, explaining that the president of Bangladesh was visiting the United States at the time and everyone flew in to meet with him. "My mom's big brothers are political figures in Bangladesh," she says, pronouncing it carefully: po-li-ti-cul. "My mom was here for a year or something, but then went back to Bangladesh and my dad came to visit, and he liked her. So they talked. He talked to my mom's big brother. My mom was, like, fourteen or fifteen when they got married," she says.

"Oh my God," Sadia exclaims. "That's young!" She is fifteen.

"Is it weird that that seems so young to you, but for your parents it was OK?"

"My mom got married when she was eighteen," Sadia corrects me.

"OK, but I think eighteen is really young," I say.

"But it's legal," Sadia points out.

"My mom still played with dolls when she got married," Nishat adds. "There's a doll my dad bought her, it's still in my room."

"That's really young," Sadia says again.

"But Sadia, you spend a lot of time caring for your nieces," I say. "So you, at a really early age, are doing some of the same work that moms do."

"I don't think it's the same. I play with them and stuff," she says. "Their moms do a lot of work. Kids are really fun to play with. But that doesn't mean I'm going to get married at a young age. If you're getting married at fourteen, fifteen, you're a kid yourself. How are you going to take care of somebody else?" Sadia asks.

"Well, Nishat's mom does a pretty good job," I say.

"In Bangladesh there are a lot of places where people get married really young. Nine, eight. It's illegal but the parents still do it. Because they get married at such a young age, these girls are illiterate. They can't really do anything about it," Sadia says.

By now we are seated and eating our mishti. The girls begin talking about their favorite parts of Bengali culture, the parts they actively seek to preserve in the States: the clothes, the food, the close-knit family structure. I am thinking about how Nishat's mom is only one year older than I am, and how different my life might be if I'd married at fifteen.

———

I am told at one point that during the period leading up to and during emergency management of the city, and then while the city is under bankruptcy, founding a church becomes one of the fastest-growing businesses in Detroit. I can never track down a source for this information, although I do come across a larger than average number of churches throughout the city—most reconfigured concrete block structures, former auto-repair shops or neighborhood stores, painted over with bright crosses and labeled in script with grand, religious-sounding names. Then friends start suggesting it, naturally, as a fundraising maneuver. "We will put on punk shows but call ourselves a church," one friend explains. "I was thinking about organizing the T-shirt line as a religious organization," another friend says.

———

Sometimes, in the normal course of talking about extremely regular stuff, the neighbor girls will mention that a distant uncle has been detained at the airport for weeks over now having a beard and not matching his passport picture exactly, or that a classmate's father hasn't returned home yet, and his children, their schoolmates, miss him greatly.

———

It has become clear that Thurber is comfortable and happy at Ca-troit. If we travel elsewhere and then return to the house, he does not need any period of reentry; once he emerges from his travel kennel he is home, ready. In fact, he is so comfortable and happy there that I wonder why I am not.

———

"Honey, I am on my way to you!" my mechanic calls and sings to me once when my truck repairs have been completed. It is overly intimate and totally inappropriate, but I like it.

———

During a party I host, All Girl Metal Band becomes agitated and begins hissing at guests. I put her in my bedroom and give her a couple days to calm down, but she does not. Soon she is swip-ing at Thurber, snarling all day long, and screeching with reg-ularity. Until now she has been the sweetest-dispositioned cat I have ever seen: friendly, slightly shy, unusually warm and loving. Her only bad habit was that she liked to drink out of the toilet but was too small to reach it with her tongue, so would often fall into the bowl and then run around the house spreading toilet water. I guess that is pretty bad. But threatening to bite some-one seems worse. One night she sits outside my bedroom door, snarling, while Thurber and I are locked inside. When I open the door in the morning, she attacks me and draws blood. I put her down. This murder costs $133.

———

One downside to the paucity of media in Detroit—besides the lack of jobs and absence of political or corporate accountability—is that no one appears to know what a writer on deadline looks like. Folks seem to think that I occasionally refuse to leave my house for days on end, stewing in the same ripped-up sweatpants, letting my hair go wild, for no reason. Even in Cambodia the tuk-tuk drivers got used to my writing binges. When I would emerge from the front gates of my apartment or hotel or dorm, they would greet me with a laugh. "Deadline!" they would say, even if it was one of only a handful of English words they knew. In Detroit, my neighbors just look at me with concern and pity or ask what happened to my other clothes.

———

Shortly after I move to town, I receive a flyer advertising a neighborhood event. When the children start mentioning the same event, I become curious because they seem to be describing it with a combination of unrelated words.

"Nishat, what is a marshmallow drop?" I ask one day, and she explains that it is an event where they drop marshmallows, as if I had asked something stupid. I withhold further questions.

On the day of the event, several friends and I attend. We find toys and games and food and adults dressed like dogs and clowns, inciting the children to engagement. Local politicians use the event to shake hands with voters. Booths are set up to distribute information. At a certain point, the children start running toward a gate that encloses a wide-open field, and soon a functionary emerges to open the gate and stand near a giant pile of boxes. Then a loud noise comes from overhead, and the kids start screaming. A military-grade helicopter flies low in the sky, hovering for a moment over all of our heads, before dropping hundreds of marshmallows to the ground, where they are eaten, or trampled, or collected and returned to the woman standing near the boxes, who accepts marshmallows in trade for a backpack. The backpack, she tells me, was supposed to be filled with products for dental hygiene, but the city couldn't get any donated, so the backpacks are instead filled with candy. She tells me this as if they are the same, toothbrushes and chocolate bars, floss and sugar wafers, and then she hands me a backpack. On the helicopter's final pass, Sadia's younger brother takes a ridiculous, comedic dive, attempting to retrieve an out-of-reach marshmallow, and bystanders applaud. A local politician comes by to congratulate himself on the successful event. "Isn't this great?" he asks me. "Plus, they're halal!" He pops a marshmallow in his mouth. I remain uncomfortable with an event that urges young people to enthusiastically greet American military vehicles.

———

"It's a good engine," my mechanic says of my pickup truck. I am gradually upgrading it, or saving it from entropy, so bring it in for repairs every few months. His inappropriate endearments have become habit, comfortable. "How much you pay for this?"

I tell him.

He nods approvingly. "You have the truck instinct," he says.

I beam.

———

It's Eid tomorrow, so the woman across the street has located a henna artist to do mehndi for all the women on the block. I am nearly dying of excitement. The neighbor girls have twice done my mehndi, and they are great at it, but this feels somehow official, a mehndi party, with food and guests and entertainment.

The artist, my neighbor's cousin, is brought in from a different part of town (several blocks away) and she is famous around these parts for her designs. Soon the porch is filled with ten, twelve, fifteen people of all ages: getting or receiving henna drawn on to their arms or feet or hands in fantastical designs, standing awkwardly away from others during the looooong drying process, eating dates, holding babies, sharing fried foods, making coffee, swapping stories, updating folks on their lives.

How can I explain what it is like, to sit at the foot of a woman so skilled she can cover my arm in flowers and nagas and archways and flourishes with liquid so thoughtlessly that she is also flipping through an iPad with her elbow at the same time? She makes no mistakes except one time when a toddler bangs into her arm, smashing the hand with which she was drawing with his entire tiny body. The mistake is swiftly cleared away by paper towel, cleverly applied.

"The hard part is drying," the mechanical engineering student next to me says, who is so pretty I cannot help but think that she should star in children's books. "I have henna everywhere. Sheets. Scarves. Every piece of clothing. It is part of the process."

I am interested in her style strategy. "Do you choose a design to match your Eid dress or just find one you like?" I ask when she sits down and flips open her computer to a gorgeous full-sleeve design she's about to request. "It all ends up matching, somehow," she says.

The next day is also the Fourth of July. I spend the day bedecked head to toe in red, white, and blue, a giant tangle of flowers and arches and swirls running up my arm, feeling more American than I ever have before.

———

There's a gas leak at the hospital and all the doctors are falling ill, but they aren't canceling appointments. My doctor, annoyed to be inviting the already sick into her office to become even sicker, asks, "Do people really care about making money more than they do human lives?"

———

My favorite new Banglatown find is Car Part House. Various car parts, fairly well organized, are left on the lawn of the house around the corner. I find a guy hauling off a whole bumper one day, and another day someone drops off a carburetor.

––––––

My daily exercise for one whole winter is walking the mile and a half to the neighborhood recreation center at various times that I am assured it will be open and finding it closed, and then walking home. It is very cool, I think every day, for a city to have a private-gym alternative. However, it is not so cool if you can never get into it. Eventually I trade in this exercise routine, of walking to the gym to discover it closed and returning home, for a series of futile attempts to build exercise machines that I order online.

––––––

For the first time, I am invited to participate in a blessing ceremony because I am a member of the community and not for any other reason, such as that I am an interesting guest or should try a certain food or to answer questions about fencing. The aim of the gathering, Nishat explains, is to ensure good luck, health, and happiness for everyone who attends, and her family would like to extend these greetings to certain individuals in particular. In fact, on the evening of the gathering, we must wait on certain neighbors so that they will also be blessed. That the event is held on American Thanksgiving is sheer coincidence, Nishat says, and anyway no one likes the taste of turkey, Sadia adds. I am dressed appropriately, arrive early enough that I can come through the front door causing the men only minor inconvenience, and everyone in attendance has seen me at these functions often enough that they do not think me an oddity or question my presence. Nishat's mom has covered the interior of her house with brightly colored bedsheets, and folks cram on couches, in chairs, and across the floor in quiet chitchat, conveying the seriousness of the occasion. The ceremony begins, and the imam sing-chants a few phrases, and everyone, except me, answers. (Sadia will later assure me that this part of the ceremony can be quite beautiful if the men participate more enthusiastically than they do now.) Then there is a period in which everyone holds their hands in front of their faces, palms open, as if about to drink rainwater, and the prayers begin in earnest.

During these prayers I think about how lucky I am to know these people, as a community and as individuals, and how fortunate I feel that they allow me to participate in such events, despite the fact that I clearly know nothing about religions or deities or other people's belief systems. But in this moment, my extensive but distanced respect for Muslim culture turns into love.

When the prayer ends, we are served food—curries, salads, rice—and Sadia, Nishat, and I go into the bedroom to eat so they can complain about YouTubers and look at their cell phones without parental oversight.

———

"ANNE!" the six-year-old across the street screams from the porch one day when I emerge from the house. "WE'RE SITTING AROUND LIKE NORMAL PEOPLE READING BOOKS!" she continues, waving one such object at me.

———

My mechanic wants to know if I will be having car trouble in July or August? He would like to take a vacation.

———

I am corralled into a social engagement with a visiting PhD student in the English department at the University of Chicago who is staying for two nights in nearby Ferndale. Eating dinner in Hamtramck, she relays to me a long story about Detroit's successful revitalization and how great it is for Detroit residents. I ask if she has ever been to Detroit before, and she admits that she has not. I point out that she has still not actually been in Detroit yet, only Ferndale and Hamtramck, two totally different cities. I ask if she intends to spend any time in Detroit, but she is so enthusiastic about the city's turnaround that she feels no need to test its veracity.

The next day I find myself thinking about her. I feel I should be annoyed with her easy spread of misinformation and disinterest in facts, but instead I am filled with longing for a hopefulness so deep that no verification is required.

———

A man involved in a political organization I like asks me if I know any women who write about capitalism. He has recently attended my book launch, for my book about women and disease and capitalism, and in fact holds a copy of this book while he speaks to me. Perhaps it has reminded him of the topic, but he has not yet connected the topic of conversation to the topic of the book in his hand. He explains that he is looking for a woman to invite to speak to the political organization, because so often the speakers are men.

I say yes and wait for him to realize what is happening and invite me to speak to the group. He does not, so I explain that I am in the middle of a national tour speaking on this precise topic, only back in town for a few days. But that I would be happy to discuss the matter with him when my tour ends.

His mannerism changes then, and he appears bored, as I have diverged from the conversation at hand. Later he emails, asking again if I can give him the names of any women who write about capitalism. It is the week my book is nominated for a national award, and I do not respond.

————

At a neighborhood arts festival, I burst into a theater by accident and then, because I am wearing my sunglasses, pause for a moment to allow my focus to adjust in the low light. The festival has been fun but not challenging, and I am deciding to head home just as a group of grade school kids clamber on stage. I panic. What if they perform? Unfortunately my eyes are still adjusting so moving is perilous. Then the emcee bounces up to the microphone to introduce the group, and pleads earnestly with us to enjoy the music because they have written it themselves and, he says, "worked really hard on it."

It is not uncommon to be induced to enjoy something in earnest that is actually insufferable. Every part of my body bristles at the emotional trap and prepares to bolt, but to do so now would actually be shitty, a needless insult to these kids, who can see me from their spot on the stage, even if I can't quite make out what is directly in front of me. I resolve to stay put until their act is over.

They begin singing. DOO-WOP. I am shocked, transported. I realize in wonder that these kids have been writing, choreographing, and rehearsing doo-wop songs after school for many months. They dispel all my reservations about Detroit's contemporary art scene in one moment. I jump up and down for joy.

———

Two people's cars were egged last week, if the current edition of the *Hamtramck Review* police blotter is to be believed. Several residents have complained that their garbage cans were overturned in the night. Otherwise, things in Hamtramck are quiet.

———

My garden is the only place I feel whole and centered. This by itself is not interesting and is something that gardeners say all the time, so it is also trite. In my garden, however, I am forced every day to pull a living thing out of the earth and kill it so that something else I like better for any number of spurious, fungible reasons—it tastes good, I like the way it looks, it makes pretty bugs come more often, or it makes other things grow better without adding extra labor for me—may thrive. I feel a tiny bit of guilt about this, throughout the day, even though it is part of learning to trust your instincts as a grower and set boundaries for yourself as a human. But sometimes the guilt stacks up, and I catch myself thinking, God, all I'm really doing is condemning stuff to death that doesn't please me.

———

One day Nishat and her mother stop by, a young woman some-where between their ages in tow. This new person wants to see the house. Nishat and her mom often bring visitors by to see my house, so I think nothing of it. But this young woman's questions grow increasingly specific. She used to live here, Nishat soon ex-plains. Her father, it turns out, built the addition that I now use as a studio when she was born. I become very excited and ask her about how the house was decorated, what she remembers about the woodwork, whether or not the floors were original, what the upstairs looked like. And then I remember. "Was your kitchen floor a black-and-white checkerboard pattern?" I scroll through my phone to find pictures of the flooring I dug out of the back, finally disposed of at the city dump.

"Yes," she says, "that was our floor. I was just a baby so I looked at it a lot."

———

After becoming ill, and then while navigating a new town as an adult, I begin to develop a very different notion of community than the one I honed after grad school. Community is the people who show up. Invited or not, desirable or not, it can only be defined as the folks who spend time with you. Perhaps you can divide various communities into different categories based on specific shared interests—a spiritual community, a creative community, a professional community—but all are defined by the people who show up.

———

Toward the end of my time in Detroit, an acquaintance comes over for tea. I explain my frustrations with the organization and describe how these have contributed to my frustrations with the city. I believe at the time that this is a one-way influence: that my anger and disappointment have made me slow to trust new people in the city.

"Oh," this acquaintance says. "I wish I'd known how frustrating this was for you."

I wasn't hiding it, I explain, but I also didn't have many people around to talk to about it.

"Well," she says, "I guess that's partially our fault. A bunch of us decided before you came that we probably couldn't trust anyone associated with [the organization]." She says it to underscore how clear it was to her that the organization had trampled on the toes of locals, but what I hear is: you have been lonely here because we ostracized you.

———

On a panel, all four winners of free houses are asked about our experiences in Detroit and whether it's our first time living in the Midwest. Nandi, who is from Detroit, and I, who moved from Chicago, look at each other. Liana and Casey give standard responses: yes, it's their first time living in the Midwest and the people are so great! But Nandi and I go deeper. She talks about growing up in the city and watching it change in multiple ways. She describes the decision to go to school in Indiana and what keeps her bound to the region. I describe how the city is similar to, and how it differs from, other midwestern cities I have lived in, but quibble with the description of Detroit as midwestern. I am thinking of time zones: Detroit chose to be in the eastern standard time zone specifically to distinguish itself from Chicago's central standard time and to better align itself with New York. I respect that. I have always found Chicago's bedtime to come distressingly early. Also I am thinking of "midwestern" as a synonym for conservative or traditional or worse: Regressive or wrong-headed. Cows and gingham. I describe how I have lived in the Midwest for most of my life but have never been labeled a midwesterner or midwestern writer, how when people try to place my work, they often ask why I left New York. To me, the idea that Detroit may have found a way to exempt itself, or extricate itself, from midwesternness is part of its appeal, a thrilling project of self-definition.

"Anybody who doesn't think of Detroit as the Midwest is racist," Nandi says flatly.

———

The mechanic calls me every few weeks to see how my truck is holding up. Once he stops by my house, where he has come to pick me up when repairs have been completed on previous occasions, just to see if everything is OK. I've given him comic books for his kids and for a while, we have a nice bond. He recommends Lebanese restaurants to me, and I suggest other reading material for his daughter. Then one day he returns my truck completely empty of the full tank of gas I'd just bought, all the seats pushed back as far as they will go, beer bottles in every crevice, some broken, dirt covering every inch of the cab's interior.

"Can you explain to me what happened here?" I ask, but I never receive an answer.

———

Approximately eighteen months since we last discussed them, Sadia asks one day if I remember the kittens that used to live in the garage of the six-year-old across the street. I tell her that I do, although I remind her that I had never actually seen them. Sadia grows very quiet. After a moment she says, "I have to tell you something." She is measured, watching me. "I killed them."

Sadia tells me that she and the other girls were worried about the kittens because they were covered in dirt, and gave them a bath. Then the kittens got cold and quiet and did not move again, she says. She is more worried about what I will say next than she is that she is a cat murderer, more worried, in other words, that I will think she is a cat murderer than that she may actually be one.

"Oh, Sadia," I tell her, "they were already sick if they were covered in dirt. I don't think the kittens had a very good chance in that garage. Maybe next time we don't give them a bath, but I don't think they would have survived anyway."

She looks relieved, and we change the subject and discuss other matters. I do not say to her, Well, Sadia, sometimes you kill cats and it's just sad. There is nothing to be done about it.

———

One late fall evening, my neighbors invite me over for dinner. They have ordered a pizza, a rare treat, and also serve traditional Bengali food. It is surprisingly formal, and we must wait until everyone is present before we begin talking. "Family meeting," Nishat whispers to me in a serious tone. When her father takes his seat, he begins asking me questions, eventually settling into a theme that I am surprised to discover is about my apparent lack of religion. I'm confused for a moment, because I have never seen the Muslims in the neighborhood exhibit any interest in converting me. Then he says, "It is important for you to accept Jesus." He is, he explains, worried about what will become of me in the afterlife. Also, Christmas is coming, and he would like me to get a Christmas tree, because no one in the neighborhood has ever seen one up close.

8

THE HOLE

The whole of the mind must lie wide open if we are to get the sense that the writer is communicating his experience with perfect fullness. There must be freedom and there must be peace. Not a wheel might grate, not a light glimmer. The curtains must be close drawn.

—VIRGINIA WOOLF, *A Room of One's Own*

A hole appears in my roof. At first it is small, easily mistaken for a tear in a shingle or a dark, wet leaf. A few windstorms and several heavy rains later, it is revealed to be a true hole, the definable presence of an absence.

My contract clearly states that the organization will repair any damage to or destruction of the house that is "not occasioned by the negligence or willful misconduct of Tenant," which is to say, that I did not deliberately or accidentally cause.

The hole is small, content with destroying the insulation in one corner of the mysterious second floor, first spotted from a ladder while cleaning out gutters. However, it widens quickly, fresh jagged edges appearing in the wake of every weather event. I seek estimates on a repair, hoping to find someone to get the work done while the organization figures out how to pay for it, but multiple roofers tell me that repairs are not an option. The roof is in bad shape and must be entirely replaced. A new roof, it is explained, will cost twenty thousand dollars. What is more, the hole is expanding so quickly that I must tend to the roof immediately or risk further property damage, including leakage and a brick chimney that could crumble and fall on to my neighbor's house. This neighbor, on the other side of Nishat's family, has a toddler whose bedroom is directly below the chimney. I dutifully forward this information to the organization.

Although I am several months shy of my two-year mark, and the roof damage well predates renovations—meaning that the organization understood the roof was damaged but did nothing to address it—the organization refuses to pay for a new roof and suggests I take the matter up with the insurance company. Unfortunately the insurance that the organization purchased on the house covers only fire damage.

But I do not have twenty thousand dollars, I explain to the organization, who has seen my tax forms and already knows this. The organizational representative I am speaking to suggests I take out a loan and think of it like rent. I remind this representative that the stated purpose of the organization is to free writers from rent so they can concentrate on writing. I explain that I gave up a decent-paying job in a different city and state that also offer funding opportunities to working artists, and by doing so also went without a paycheck for much of the previous year in order to uphold the organization's mission, as it is one I had hoped to see implemented on a much wider scale. I express legitimate concern that I might not be considered eligible for a loan and, given the city's meager selection of grant-making bodies and scant job opportunities in the arts, add that I'm just not convinced I could pay it back anyway.

Then the representative from the organization suggests I get a real job.

———

In 2011, the Austrian national swim team spends a day at Pompano Beach, Florida. Member Jakub Maly, nineteen, perhaps tired of swimming, relaxes by digging a massive pit in the sand. Then, thrilled by his vast creation, gets in it. Quickly the walls erode, and Maly's head is soon covered with sand. It becomes difficult for him to breathe, and the sand begins to crush him. It takes two hours and sixty rescue workers to free Maly from danger, but onlookers remain impressed by his creation, the origin of all the fuss. "It was the perfect hole," Sandra King of Pompano Beach Fire Rescue tells ABC News Radio on May 9, "until he decided to jump into it."

———

I ponder options. I'm four months away from the two-year mark, at which point I am set to receive full ownership of a house with a broken roof. What to do? Pursue a loan I can't afford only to remain tied to a city I struggle to tolerate? Or walk away from neighbors I love?

A friend and I discuss. She thinks I should leave. She is a

curator, a champion of my comics journalism collaboration with Melissa. "At least you got a great project out of it," she offers. Her logic stays with me. It's what artists do, yes? Turn crap situations into projects?

———

There are at least two horror films named *The Hole*—a dark 2001 film out of the UK starring Thora Birch and Keira Knightley and a 2009 movie by Joe Dante that's more fun than terrifying. In both films, groups of young people discover holes, and the young men, or boys, decide to enter them. *Holes* (2003) is a film about groups of boys digging holes for unknown reasons, which I have never seen, and *Hole in the Ground* (2019) features a young man who emerges from a hole and behaves unusually. The holes in our cinematic imaginary are often terrifying unknowns that appear mysteriously and which, for some reason, men and boys feel compelled to enter. Then, commonly, they get stuck, or grabbed, or possessed. And when the young men emerge—for they always do—they are permanently changed. The hole has had a profound impact upon them, wizened them. The sexual metaphor is trite and sad.

———

I do not start writing this book the moment I move into the house but at the moment it becomes clear I may never be able to move out of it. At the height of my frustration I consider abandoning the building, just walking away, instead of relying on the services of building contractors and lawyers in order to put it on the market and watch it fail to sell, because why would anyone move to a city that doesn't function and has no jobs?

During this time I meet a man at a party who makes problems like this disappear, an arsonist. I tell him I am not interested in his services, and he says he understands but that if I become interested, his services cost x amount of dollars. He tells me some of the houses he's worked on, and later I search for news stories about them online but find nothing. His résumé therefore seems impressive. The main problem with hiring him is that I have canceled my insurance and no longer have coverage from which I might benefit in case of a fire. There are other downsides too. In truth, the only thing to be gained by burning my house down is that it would never be anyone's problem again. That's when the literary instinct kicks in. "Or I could just make this everyone's problem," I think. Then I start writing this book.

———

I meet with a four-year-old over breakfast with his novelist father in New York. The very young man agrees, sight unseen, to do some contracting work on my house, negotiating me down from paying him three dollars to paying him zero dollars at a rapid clip. He does not ask what contracting is, nor does he inquire about any of the specifics of the project, but he seems pretty trustworthy and I'm swayed by his confidence. His father urges him to raise his bid, explaining that roof installation is difficult and dangerous and materials expensive. His father points out that a zero-dollar price tag is a pretty good deal for me but not a very good deal for him. My new contractor will not budge. "I set the price," he announces to the table, "and I want zero dollars."

———

If you come across a hole in South Dakota, the very last thing on earth you should do is try to get in it, just FYI. If it's not a rattlesnake den, which it probably is, it's likely the nest of a bald eagle, unsure of where else to sleep in the absence of trees, and disturbing it is a federal offense. Still, while I am there directing a summer camp for at-risk youth, I have to tell both boy campers and male counselors on an almost daily basis, "Stay out of the holes."

I come to think of it as a masculine trait, to see a hole and try to get all up in it instead of what you should do, which is leave immediately.

Then my own hole emerges. And what do I do.

———

I take out a loan to cover the new roof, committing myself to expenditures that exceed my income every month by the exact amount of the loan repayment. I cover the first payment by skimping on prescription medication, but then panic sets in. A week later I am offered a visiting writer position at a small liberal arts college for the following year, a three-month stint that will allow me to pay off the loan in full. I accept, but the new problems posed by such a solution are jarring: in order to afford the free house I was given in Detroit, I must—at least temporarily—live elsewhere.

———

"Some of these girls, they buy a house, they have these—excuse my French—crap ladders. You really got an eye for a good sturdy tool!" my roofer says, not even trying to get into my pants.

———

The first house Nandi Comer is promised is in my neighborhood, but this house is deemed unsalvageable a few months into the renovation process. The second house is in a different neighborhood, and Nandi spends time in the area trying to find ways to fit into the existing creative community, but money runs out to repair this house, and the new round of fundraising is slow going. As the two-year anniversary of my move-in date approaches, also the date Nandi was publicly promised a house, it is becoming increasingly clear that the organization is struggling to uphold its commitments. At first, the organization assures us it is doing all it can. Then phone calls and emails go unreturned.

———

Two years and one day after I move to Detroit, I am handed a deed to a house with my name on it by a low-level government functionary. The day is mostly about paperwork, but once my final task is complete—transferring water service to my name—I find I am four blocks away from a wine bar I like. I go there and order a single unreasonably priced glass of wine and put it on my credit card, desperate to take one small moment to celebrate this milestone. The bartender asks what is new. "I became a homeowner today," I tell him.

"Congratulations!" he says. "How does it feel?"

"It's . . . complicated," I say.

"It always is," he agrees.

Let me tell you something I don't share with a lot of people. The Detroit house is actually the second free house I am offered that year. The first is in California, and it is offered to me during a reporting trip I am invited on by a source. The story he has information on is complex, but it involves some investigative work I have been doing on human trafficking. At the center of this particular case is an alleged child rapist—wrongly accused, according to my source.

My source tells me he is working with an investigative team, and after a mutual if cursory vetting process, I am invited to LA to pick up documents necessary to craft the story for publication and meet this team. However, when my source greets me at the airport, he is alarmingly unbathed. It's my first clue that something is amiss. Then he fails to meet me at the appointed hour the next day, or at all. That's my second. The third day, I am slated to meet the investigative team, but there is a sudden change of plans and I only manage to meet with one lawyer, who pulls me aside after the meeting to ask in a hushed voice if I am OK. I am rattled by his concern, which appears sincere, and when my source suggests we go for lunch to discuss the case and the possibility of joining the investigative team, I agree because it will keep us both in public view.

He drives me to a rich suburb and, along the way, fills me in on certain details of the case: the conspiracy, the allegations, the evidence. Most of this last is piled, unbound, across the back seats of his hatchback, and the plan we had earlier agreed to was that we would leave these papers with me at my hotel that afternoon. But doubt creeps in. As we drive past restaurants I suggest we stop at—requests he ignores—panic mounts. Then he refers to the accused by a childhood nickname, surprisingly affectionate. He apologizes quickly. It was clearly an accident.

By this time we have arrived at a park, and when he gets out of the car I follow because there are more people inside the park than there are, at that moment, in the parking lot. We stand on a hill overlooking several estates, properties that sell for millions. He points out a small green house across the way, a tidy ranch with a wide yard and a two-car garage, in front of which is parked a Jaguar and a BMW. "This is why I brought you here," he says with an air of solemnity. "If you agree to stay and join the team, that house is yours."

I barely register the house because I am recalibrating every interaction I have had with this man in light of his slipup. I am piecing together that the lawyer we met with earlier was not defending the accused as I had been informed, but merely advising on the case, and that the alleged rapist was somehow either related to my source or a childhood friend. More alarming was my dawning awareness that, since my source appeared incapable of understanding that I had withheld consent on a majority of the day's activities, I could no longer trust his assessment of the accused's guilt or innocence. What I was realizing was that I was now likely standing in the presence of the best friend of a child rapist, who was asking me earnestly to devote my life to ensuring the freedom of someone who did not deserve it in exchange for an extremely expensive house. That's when he makes another slipup. He refers to our outing as a date.

Anyway, I tell you this because there are still days when it is not clear to me that I chose the correct free house.

———

I attempt to locate insurance that might offer me protection in case of damage or natural disaster, but beyond the type of insurance I already had, revealed to be useless and canceled, my house, it turns out, is uninsurable. The reasons for this are many. The exterior door to what used to be the second floor, now boarded and inaccessible, is considered some kind of fire hazard, and the vinyl siding stolen from the back of the house while it was still being renovated is deemed a liability. To make the house insurable, I would have to install railings along the perimeter of the concrete slab in the back, previously a garage floor.

Then there is the redlining. Most companies, I discover, will not insure homes in my neighborhood at all, allowing those that do to set exorbitant prices. The systematic denial of services by government, banks, and private companies to neighborhoods with a high proportion of minority residents is usually done off book, but when I meet face-to-face with a friendly, white insurance agent, she acknowledges why she can't sell me home insurance. "It's the redlining," she says.

The total cost estimate for repairs to my house that will allow me to insure it—without including the costs of the insurance itself—rises so quickly past the ten-thousand-dollar mark that I give up on the idea. Twenty thousand dollars for a free house is enough.

———

I consult a lawyer, who after reviewing the case is eager to put together a lawsuit. "Well," I hem, "the thing is, the organization doesn't have any money."

"Ah," he says. "Now you're thinking like a lawyer." Suing people is not really about determining who is right, he says. It is about whether or not the parties responsible possess the means to be held responsible by a court of law.

But this situation is slightly more complicated. Suing the organization for funds to cover my roof replacement would further delay Nandi's house.

———

I fall into depression. I can no longer envision an achievable future for myself in which I am happy. I snap at everyone, humans and cats. I eat bad food, stop tending the garden, can't read. Although I have been sad before, the quality of this episode is particular. I am despondent and angry at all hours, sleeping poorly. My blood pressure elevates, then elevates again. Then, because I have multiple degenerative diseases for which there are no known cures, both physical pain and mental anguish deepen quickly. One hazard of chronic illness is that confronting medical reality often creates emotional distress. This is not terribly concerning to the medical profession, however, which acknowledges that one of the leading causes of death for people with autoimmune disease is suicide. Soon I am pondering death scenarios of my own devising.

We talk about depression as a hole, a deep pit in the ground, and the metaphor suits my mood: the unending lowness, the crystalline darkness, the sharp steepness that keeps me in place and feels impossible to climb.

Then one night I receive an email inquiring if I am interested in a permanent job back in Chicago. A month later I am gone.

9

THE HOMEOWNER

It is far more important at the moment to know how
much money women had and how many rooms than
to theorise about their capacities.

—VIRGINIA WOOLF, *A Room of One's Own*

The timeline is this. On May 3, 2018, I complete all required paperwork, meet with all relevant notaries public, visit all the proper offices in the correct order, and am handed a deed to the house I have lived in for exactly two years and one day. Nearly immediately, I take out a loan and replace the roof.

In September, I am offered a job in Chicago. The following month, I move into an apartment and return on weekends to prepare the Detroit house for sale. In December, I locate a realtor, and we agree to list the house on the market in the spring.

On January 3, 2019, the title agency—the entity that, in Michigan, facilitates the paperwork of any real estate transaction—calls with bad news. The organization is "not in good standing with the State of Michigan," the title agent tells me over the phone. I am not surprised to hear this, although I have no real idea what it means or why it would matter to me. Probably taxes, he suggests. But to proceed with the sale of the house, the organization will need to file all proper paperwork and clear up any remaining concerns directly with the state. They could owe money, paperwork may be misfiled, or there could be some other problem, he says. The point is, he clarifies, I can't sell the house until they clean up their act. I'm immediately concerned—the only communications I have received from the organization in eight months are fundraising emails—but a board member steps in and manages the process. By Valentine's Day, the organization is again in good standing with the state, and the title agency gives me the OK to proceed with the listing.

On March 15, convinced that my final hurdle has been surmounted, I place the remainder of my belongings in Detroit into storage. The house goes on the market. There are several showings right away, some quite promising. As interest rises, we prepare paperwork for a sale and do a title search on the property, usually a formality to ensure all documents are in order for a clean transfer of ownership.

The name listed on the title as the owner of my house is not my own.

———

Nishat tells me one day that when she was little, really little, a woman moved into my house. Maybe with a man. They were loud, Nishat says, but nice. She does not say much else about them, which leads me to assume they were Black. Then one day they were gone. They left a dog in the front bedroom closet, Nishat explains, and animal control was called to liberate it. The dog was scared, hungry, and angry, she describes. Telling the story makes her angry, too.

"Are you sure?" I ask, surprised. Her timeline would place people in my house around 2010, 2011—which doesn't match up with what I had been told by the organization, that the house sat abandoned for eight years, that in 2008 whoever had been living in it just picked up and left. This had made sense: financial crisis, rock-bottom employment in the city. It can be more costly to attempt to sell a house than to pick up and leave it with whatever you can carry. The house narrated its own story from there. There was a fire at some point, presumably during this period of abandonment, because the interior roof beams are still black and charred. The kitchen renovations occurred much earlier, since the abandoned linoleum is buried under eight years of mulberry overgrowth. I also know there was a push to preserve the house after the fire, instead of demolish it, because an organizer who argued on its behalf sends me a promotional flyer describing the effort. Above all, I am relying on the word of the organization, which had assured me that the house was abandoned, not seized in foreclosure, although my subsequent investigations into foreclosure for the comics series with Melissa have uncovered no clear legal distinction between an abandoned home and a foreclosed one. Is there an official process for declaring a home abandoned? Unclear. Why would there be? It is not a question I know to ask as I move in. In the moment, I trust what the organization has told me: that it has successfully avoided capitalizing on the foreclosure crisis.

Perhaps the bafflement on my face reads as anger to sensitive Nishat. She clams up then, never one to contradict an elder.

———

Loveland Technologies, a data-based mapping project in Detroit, finds that 111,167 of the nearly four hundred thousand properties in the city went into foreclosure between 2002 and 2014. Similarly, the Moratorium NOW! Coalition to Stop Foreclosures, Evictions, and Utility Shutoffs in Michigan notes that one in every three homes within city limits was foreclosed between 2005 and 2015. Some of these were mortgage foreclosures, in which a home buyer defaults on a loan from a bank, and the bank seizes the property. But Detroit's foreclosure crisis is unique for its excessively high rate of property tax foreclosures, in which a home is seized by a governmental body after three years of unpaid property taxes. The distinction between the two forms of foreclosure is important and telling: mortgage foreclosures are enacted by banks, by companies. Property tax foreclosures are the result of laws created under a democracy and enacted by elected officials. A stunning one in four homes in Detroit, according to Moratorium NOW!, were foreclosed between 2011 and 2015 for unpaid property taxes.

———

It can be helpful to think about property ownership not as a description of one's legal relationship with an object—in this case, a house I was given—but as a series of rights one holds against any- one else who may wish to take, damage, destroy, misuse, or profit from the object in question. Laws, after all, can only ever gov- ern the actions of people. Thus the various documents involved in home ownership confer different rights on the supposed owner but only collectively can be said to constitute anything resembling what we think of as "home ownership." Take the difference be- tween a deed and a title, for example. Deeds grant the right to own a property, turns out, and are documents used to transfer title. A title, however, grants the right to a property itself.

So it is no small matter when a title search reveals an in- consistency. No matter what other paperwork may be in order, unclear titles legally invalidate the presumption of ownership. In many cities, title inconsistencies trigger alarm, and real estate law firm associates are dispatched to research precedents and case law.

In Detroit, there is a process, a guy to call. A lawyer who fixes title disputes within six months for $1,200 in something called a quiet title action, the legal means of quelling disputes regarding property rights. I never lay eyes on this lawyer. The title agency hires him. Apparently they work with him a lot.

"Couldn't you have just not hired him?" friends ask later. But options in this case are few: I can clear the title myself in a quiet title action; abandon the property and allow the county to fore- close or sell to a disreputable investor, in both cases pushing off the quiet title process to a future owner; or stay in the house until I die, when I will no longer care.

———

Until now, my experience of winning a free house has been marked by the keen difference between how great that sounds and the reality of what it means in Detroit. I think often of Woolf's description of London: "We were all being shot backwards and forwards on this plain foundation to make some pattern." I like the implied trust that beneath the experience of chaos might lie a benevolent, at least undamaging, force, and the extremely modernist visual. But any such trust I had—in the city, in the organization—has evaporated, any neat pattern with it. When people ask how I came to be living in Detroit, a question I am asked there more often than any place else I have ever lived, I now answer, "An organization gave me a free house, but it turns out they didn't own it. They gave me somebody else's house."

———

The name listed on the title, T—— L——, and previous address—also mine—allow me to start searching for information on the internet. Facebook gives me nothing, as the name is not uncommon, but a cursory records search turns up a mid-forties woman and a host of affiliated individuals that do and do not share her last name. With three data points—name, address, likely relatives—I can conduct a search for public records. The site I use charges a steep fee and occasionally halts its process to ask if I believe the person for whom I am searching may have a criminal record or a secret online dating profile. Users of this service are often conducting background checks or looking for catfishers, but I don't care whom she dates or how she gets by.

What I want to know is why she left her house and whether or not she wants it back.

———

On April 24, 2019, a civil lawsuit is filed in my name by a lawyer I never meet. I am the plaintiff and T—— L—— the defendant. "Plaintiff, Anne Elizabeth Moore, has an ownership interest in a parcel of real property located in the County of Wayne, State of Michigan," reads the Complaint to Quiet Title, filed as part of the quiet title action my title agency has solicited on my behalf. I am not alerted in advance to the particularities of the quiet title process; I have merely paid for a service and the service is being performed. When I later read details of the lawsuit I brought against a woman who may already have been under financial duress, I am aghast at the easy slide from celebrated home ownership—the public gift of a free house!—to the call for state interference in perceived threats to that claim. Admittedly, I feel less anguish about it since she does not reside on the property. But still.

———

Nestled within my court documents are important details: On February 1, 2010, a man named W—— M—— sells my house to T—— L—— for seven hundred dollars. The property is foreclosed on September 12, 2012, and reverted to the Wayne County Treasurer's Office. On February 7, 2013, for the sum of zero dollars, the house is sold to the Planning and Development Department of the City of Detroit, and on February 17, 2015, it is sold again, by the Detroit Land Bank Authority to the organization, for five thousand dollars.

The steps of a property tax foreclosure are clear, and listed on the website of the Wayne County Treasurer's Office. In brief, the process takes a minimum of three years, which by my estimation would have T—— L—— notified of imminent foreclosure no earlier than September 2012 and the house foreclosed in September 2013. Only after that would she lose all rights to the house, which would then be available for sale to the land bank. So the timeline seems off for a legal property tax foreclosure, although a mortgage foreclosure on a seven-hundred-dollar real estate purchase is even more unlikely.

Wholly absent from the court documents I receive is any indication that T—— L—— was notified of the county's decision to foreclose, a necessary step highlighted multiple times on the treasurer's office website. For obvious reasons, not only should a property owner be notified if their property is being revoked, but this notification must be documented, provable. Failing to document notification of a foreclosure could be viewed as a skipped step in the foreclosure process, a mere paperwork hassle the county simply overlooked. However, it is just as valid to say that T—— L——'s property was illegally seized by Wayne County, who gave it to the city to sell for five thousand dollars.

———

The civil suit filed in my name in April necessitates a summons be issued to T—— L—— at that same time. "In the name of the people of the State of Michigan," the document explains, "you are being sued." A month later, another document outlines attempts by the state to find a current address for T——L——, including internet searches undertaken, telephone books consulted, and official requests made to the post office for change-of-address forms. Seven years late, these documents outline the level of scrutiny that should have been used to notify T——L——at the time of foreclosure.

An included affidavit describes the process server's subsequent attempts to serve T—— L——. It reads, "On April 27, at 9:00 a.m., Personal Service and Summons and complaint was attempted [on the Defendant at address] and at that time and place, a man answered the door and stated the Defendant is not known there." Two further attempts are made at this address, but no one answers the door to the process server again.

Three attempts are made at another address associated with T—— L——, beginning on May 4, 2019, although no one ever answers the door there. "Process Server could see inside and there was no furniture inside," the document notes.

————

Absent any appearance by T—— L——, and following the process server's failure to locate her, a judge orders the summons be delivered by first-class mail, and that notification of the summons appear in the *Detroit Legal News* for three consecutive weeks. In June, a notarized affidavit of publication is filed with the Wayne County court.

It's in keeping with the legal fiction that making legal notices available for public review allows for public awareness—the structure that upholds the notion that ignorance of the law is no defense—but it's still odd, anachronistic. Does anyone really read the *Detroit Legal News*? Can former homeowners be presumed to check it weekly, years after vacating a residence? And is the publication of text a reliable means of conveying legal matters in a city with a public schools system in which the fundamental right to read is under dispute?

––––––

As a person with several chronic diseases that each manifest as pain in various parts of my body, I have come to recognize a sense of disembodiment, an untethering that occurs when extreme sensation sets in. I feel in these moments as if I am connected to the present only by a single long rope from the gut, perhaps an intestine slipped loose, while my sense of self floats away, distant and remote. I can perceive events as they unfold, manipulate limbs in emulation of reaction, but my mind is away, calculating. Between my thinking self and my physical self is a white-hot barrier I don't dare to cross. Learning to cross it anyway is what therapists and pain management specialists call "being present to pain." It is extremely difficult to sit in full-body agony and allow yourself to feel it until the agony passes, but it is a necessary step in the healing process.

––––––

If I were to craft a composite portrait of Detroiters I have come to know, I would sketch out a strong, steady woman of color who conserves her energy in public to ensure she retains enough to get through the day, focused always on the survival of her children. She would be kept with some regularity from opportunity by municipal failure or malfeasance, making instead do with what is on hand, parceling it to loved ones carefully, often well aware of the lead poisoning, the crumbling public school, the absence of books from library shelves, the water shutoff, the foreclosure. The women I meet in Detroit maintain an entire city on the strength of love and perseverance. That Detroit continues to exist at all is because these women stay and care for their children. In the absence of any other information about her, I come to see T—— L—— as such a woman. I suppose I could be wrong.

———

In the final days of the quiet title process, an unknown party emerges to claim ownership of my house. Not T—— L——, not the organization, none of the previously listed title holders, in fact. Someone new. The title agency suggests that a real estate speculator is probably just making a false claim to the property. The agent tells me not to worry, that it will be dispelled soon enough, that he sees this all the time.

It is, however, the last straw. I respond via email with a sharply worded note containing links to several newspaper articles, documentary films, radio appearances, and clips from local and national newscasts that document and even celebrate my receipt of the house and suggest these be forwarded to the court. I demand the judge ask the unknown party why nobody contested fucking ownership of the house when it was publicly awarded to me three and a half years beforehand. When it could have saved us all a lot of time.

A few days later, the unknown party's complaints are dismissed.

———

The Default Judgment to Quiet Title is entered on September 6, 2019. T—— L——'s interests "and the interest(s) of her devisees, successors and assigns in the property legally . . . are extinguished," the document reads. The house, in other words, is now mine. Five and a half years after I am first told I will be given one.

———

If this were a hard-boiled detective novel, I'd knock off for the day with some whiskey and go bed some dame. I do neither, although I do pet my cat enthusiastically and eat a particularly extravagant green salad.

———

No one can be truly excited about the outcome of a multiyear struggle, only relieved, I think, and there is often little reward regardless of stakes but the chance to move on. The loss of energy and resources is always to be mourned; the grief of destroyed expectations and broken promises seems to have no end. Deep sorrow without a death, or the loss of a relationship, always strikes me as odd, unsupportable. Nevertheless, once I become a home-owner I am filled with despair and bafflement.

I contact the lawyers hired by my title agency to perform the quiet title action and request copies of all relevant legal documents. "I'm writing a book," I explain to an uninterested secretary, who forwards the files months later. It is only then that I read what has been done in my name, services I paid for. What I did. That sense of disembodiment kicks in then, the tethered distancing. It is not physical pain that unmoors me, but something more like psychic distress at the ease with which I participated in a fundamentally violent process, the seizure of property, part of a structure in-tended to ensure folks like me have and retain access to wealth, and folks like T——— L——— do not.

———

Bloomberg News publishes an article on August 21, 2013, claiming that Detroit is overrun with wild dogs—around fifty thousand of them, the piece estimates wildly. When the unsubstantiated rumor spreads, the public has evidence, however false, that the city has gone feral. A Michigan State University (MSU) study published February 3, 2014, downgrades the estimate to a more believable 7,500 strays but, more interesting, reveals how severely understaffed the City of Detroit is as it prepares to emerge from bankruptcy. MSU finds that there are only four officers in the animal control division—although the city, the report notes, pledges to hire more.

The severe understaffing of city services isn't just limited to animal control, however, or to the period of emergency management. A year after emerging from bankruptcy, local NPR affiliate WDET in late 2015 reports that the police department is still underfunded and understaffed. Little seems to change with time. In 2018 I'm told that the City of Detroit's Office of the Assessor has only two employees, and this is one reason offered for the slow implementation of new property tax assessment procedures. In 2019, when a nine-year-old girl is mauled and killed by stray dogs, lack of capacity at animal control is blamed once again.

Given the chronic understaffing that continues today, one can't help but wonder how many people were employed to notify residents during the period between 2011 and 2015, when a quarter of all housing stock in the city was in property tax foreclosure, and whether these employees were paid well enough to ensure that they properly fulfilled the duties of their jobs.

———

When seventy-year-old Antoinette Coleman finally pays off her thirty-year mortgage, she fails to notice that property taxes, previously rolled into her monthly bank payments, begin to arrive separately. She falls behind on payments, and in 2017 her home is seized in foreclosure by the Wayne County treasurer for a back debt of $291, Sarah Alvarez writes in *Bridge Magazine* on May 17, 2018.

In-person notification of property tax foreclosure appears to be rare in Detroit. Most residents say that the first sign of foreclosure is a yellow bag tacked to a front door. "But the following notifications of the status of the home [are] ambiguous and easy to ignore," writes Andrea Perez of *The Michigan Daily* on September 11, 2018. "Many don't comprehend the severity of their situation due to the legal jargon and confusing format of the notifications," the article continues.

"I started to read them," one man facing eviction explains to Perez, "and I was like I seen October you know and that's how they do it in bold, so it makes you think you have until October. I'm looking at the papers then I read down below in the writing and I'm like, 'Oh wow.'"

In 2015, according to the Minnesota Center for Fiscal Excellence annual study of property tax rates, *50-State Property Tax Comparison Study*, Detroit has the highest effective property tax rate of any American city. Three years later, the same report finds that Detroit's ranking has fallen, although only to third place.

The degree to which cities rely on property taxes for funding, alongside property values of homes in those cities, are the two biggest factors in property tax variation throughout the country. Detroit, the 2018 report suggests, suffers from both rock-bottom property values and, in a roundabout way, sky-high reliance on property tax income.

———

Few banks offer mortgages to Detroit home buyers, so many Detroiters live in houses purchased under land contracts, private agreements in which buyers make loan repayments directly to property owners, structured somewhat differently than private mortgages, which are rare in the city. Land contracts do not transfer legal title to the buyer until they are entirely paid off—a condition that favors the seller—and are not federally regulated. They remain popular, however, because land contracts do not often require credit checks. Other disclosures are also unnecessary. Sabrina Beal purchases a home under land contract, but the seller fails to disclose that back taxes are owed on the property, debt homeowners accrue automatically on top of annual property taxes. Beal can't make the monthly payments on the back taxes, so she loses her home to property tax foreclosure in 2015, Nancy Kaffer writes in the June 21, 2019, *Detroit Free Press*.

———

All Michigan cities and townships annually sell off debts to home counties, which means that after three years of unpaid property taxes, the foreclosure process that kicks in is Wayne County's, not Detroit's. It's not typical. Michigan is one of only twelve states that allows counties to profit from the sale of property seized in tax foreclosure.

"It is akin to stealing," Larry Salzman, an attorney arguing in front of the Michigan Supreme Court that the practice should be abolished, tells Mike Wilkinson of *Bridge Magazine* for a November 9, 2019, article. "The government shouldn't be taking more than is owed to them to cure the tax deficiency," he adds, referencing cases like Antoinette Coleman's $291 shortfall. To him, the situation is clear. The takings clause of the Fifth Amendment to the United States Constitution reads, "Nor shall private property be taken for public use, without just compensation."

———

In 2014, Erica Perez accidentally underpays the property taxes on her Detroit home by $144, according to a *Detroit News* article published July 9, 2019. No one alerts her to the discrepancy until she receives a foreclosure notice three years later, after the deadline to pay off the amount—now $357, with fees and interest—has passed. The Wayne County Treasurer's Office seizes the property and sells it at auction for $108,000.

———

I meet a man facing foreclosure who does not want to give his name. He's a general laborer, born in Detroit, midsixties, tall, white, and lanky. He bought his home years back, after he spotted a foreclosure notice on his rental unit, and started leasing out a bedroom to a friend last year. The rent has been his only consistent source of income since work's dried up, he says. "I'm getting older," he admits sadly. "They don't want to give work to someone like me. They want a young guy." Last year he says he earned $1,270.

For three years, he's applied for the City of Detroit Hardship Program property tax exemption, intended to quell rising fore-closure rates and ease the financial burdens of low-income home-owners, although he says the application process is confusing. One year when he submitted an application, he says, the city told him he didn't qualify but gave no reason. There's a preliminary application form you have to fill out to receive the real application, but the office he went to said they were out of it when he went to reapply the following year. Earlier this year, he says he was told he didn't earn enough money to qualify for assistance.

His property taxes went unpaid during the three years of unsuccessful application for the hardship exemption. So unless he can pay off the back taxes, an unknown amount, the county plans to foreclose his home within weeks and sell it at auction. While the county doesn't evict tenants, a new owner likely would, which could put him out on the cold Detroit streets as early as November.

———

My research into the foreclosure crisis is undertaken, first, for the comics project. After interviews or new research I text Melissa: I just met the most amazing man! Or, You will not believe this woman's story. Or, Uh so can we work in this data set from 1963? I include pictures that she can draw from, and we discuss the arc of the story. The project is hard, because convincing people to share stories of horrible things that are happening to them for no apparent reason feels inadequate to the calamity, yet turning their stories into online comics feels productive, a way of clearly depicting injustice in relatively quick turnaround, an attempt to allow for thoughtfulness in solution-finding. Our subjects often find the process fun, and we discuss their depictions, a way for them to exert some control over a situation in which they perhaps otherwise have little. I find I rely on Melissa, who lives elsewhere, to be a calming presence, to remind me that there are places in the country where such behavior is not the norm. But when our project is complete I discover that the information is still useful, relevant to my daily life, but that I no longer have an outlet for it that feels productive, or a friend I can reasonably rely on to consider its impact. The anger builds up in my stomach, at first at the continued injustice, then at what I gradually come to see as my complicity in it.

———

A new hit pops up during my regular online search for information about T—— L——. In an article about a new Detroit public school busing program, a parent with that name proclaims the virtues of the several just-added routes. Included is a picture of a larger-set woman, wearing a pretty paisley dress, exquisitely applied eye makeup, and a perfect bun atop her head. I can't tell her age, but her hair is streaked with gray. Her child, thirteen, would have been born in 2005, and Nishat didn't recall any young kids. But maybe?

———

By 2015, Wayne County tallies more homes sold in Detroit on land contracts than under traditional mortgages, but because no requirements are in place for land contracts to be publicly filed, it is widely understood that the practice is far more common than official records indicate. In fact, land contracts and other private financing deals like lease-to-own agreements go largely unregulated, and entire companies exist to buy up foreclosed homes at auction in bulk, make no repairs to them, and offer them on land contract to interested parties. With no inspections to pass, many such properties lack amenities save walls and a roof; tenants accept responsibility to install plumbing and other necessities like hot water heaters, furnaces, or windows.

For many it seems ideal: minimal monthly payments follow deposits of only a few thousand dollars, with no landlord hovering about concerned with maintaining the value of their property. But many land contracts further stipulate an introductory period, when the purchaser is treated as a tenant, and this complicates the arrangement.

Douglas Todd had signed an agreement to rent for four months before his land contract kicked in, *The Detroit News* reports on February 29, 2016. But "after buying and installing sinks, toilets, and pipes for the house," the article explains, Todd was late with a payment. Then he got a twelve-thousand-dollar water bill, charges held over from previous occupants. He was evicted from his home before the land contract officially started.

Sellers tell *The Detroit News* that the rental period serves two purposes. It ensures the buyer is ready for the financial commitment of home ownership, for one. More important, it's easier to evict a renter than someone on a land contract. This is key if your plan is to turn over multiple renters, each convinced they've finally found their dream home.

———

After multiple conversations with survivors of Detroit's housing crisis, I grow to realize that locking a dog, or dogs, inside a property you intend to step away from for a while acts like a cheap alarm system. Property damage is minimized, interior pipes and wiring go unstripped. It's not great for the dog, of course, but it is an act undertaken to afford a homeowner protection. What I start to wonder is whether or not one would lock a dog in a home they intended to permanently abandon.

———

"No government relies on money from tax foreclosures as much as Wayne County," write Joel Kurth, Mike Wilkinson, and Laura Herberg for *Bridge Magazine* on June 6, 2017. A $22.5 million budget shortfall in 2014 was entirely erased by the seizure and sale of homes following unpaid property taxes, for example, and the article estimates another $286 million would be collected in back taxes, fees, and homes sold at auction between 2015 and 2019. The property tax foreclosure crisis, it seems, is the county's primary source of income.

In July 2020, the Michigan Supreme Court rules unanimously that selling tax-foreclosed properties for profit without compensating the former owner is unconstitutional. Although property tax foreclosures are on hold that year due to the pandemic, they are again scheduled for 2021.

———

A June 14, 2018, *Detroit News* article suggests that 10 percent of the unprecedented volume of foreclosures in the city between 2011 and 2015 were based on inflated property assessments, a problem the city has acknowledged for years.

"When we assess people honestly, a lot more start paying taxes," Mayor Mike Duggan explains at a January 2015 press conference, "which is going to mean a significant reduction in foreclosures."

He doesn't say, We have been assessing people dishonestly, taking their homes, and making the county a ton of money from the sales. But this is also true.

———

Bernadette Atuahene and Christopher Berry suggest, in their 2018 report, *Taxed Out: Illegal Property Tax Assessments and the Epidemic of Tax Foreclosures in Detroit*, that inflated assessments violate the Michigan Constitution, which states that properties cannot be assessed at more than half their market value. "Between 2009 and 2015," the authors state, "the City of Detroit assessed 55 to 85 percent of its residential properties in violation of the Michigan Constitution. Such unconstitutional assessments belie the legitimacy of Detroit's unparalleled property tax foreclosure rates."

———

In 2018, property tax foreclosures hit a fourteen-year low, with fewer than three thousand properties facing foreclosure, according to *Crain's Detroit Business*. The May 2, 2019, story states that property tax exemptions rose, and a new program offering door-to-door foreclosure education and legal referrals informed 21 percent of homeowners that were behind on their property taxes that they were delinquent. The program, Neighbor-to-Neighbor, is funded by the Quicken Loans Community Fund, itself a response to the role Quicken Loans holds in the foreclosure crisis.

According to an article by Christine MacDonald and Joel Kurth in *The Detroit News* on July 1, 2015, "Detroit-based Quicken Loans . . . had the fifth-highest number of mortgages that ended in foreclosure in Detroit over the last decade," with over half the foreclosed properties in extreme disrepair, slated for demolition, or just entering property tax foreclosure. Quicken Loans CEO Dan Gilbert, often touted as the billionaire savior of Detroit, has funded blight-removal programs that demolish low-property-value homes, in addition to providing more recent support for educational programs.

"I wish banks would spend more funds like Dan Gilbert to try to fix the mess," Brooke Tucker, an attorney for the ACLU of

Michigan, tells *The Detroit News*. "But they do have a responsibility for the mess."

———

The focus on blight in Detroit—a vague term that more or less means an unsightly house—is a political maneuver intended to guide public attention away from the root causes of foreclosure, lenders and government, to the individuals affected by it, cast as bad actors. These are people, we are told, who abdicate responsibility for property and drag down neighboring property values. The problem with such a focus is not solely one of optics, however, because blight-removal programs, including those funded by Dan Gilbert, are big-money operations.

Indeed, when the city applied for federal funds—the Hardest Hit Fund—the money was supposed to go to unemployed and underemployed residents who faced foreclosure, through ventures like the Hardship Program property tax exemption. But a November 1, 2017, report, *Improving TARP's Investment in American Workers*, notes discrepancies in the city's disbursement methods. "The Michigan state agency turned down 12,653 people who earned less than $30,000 but gave Hardest Hit Fund dollars to 1,176 people who earned more than $90,000 and 1,884 people who made between $70,000 and $89,999.... Nearly 5,000 people in the Detroit metropolitan area who earned less than $30,000 were turned down," the report states.

The money went instead to blight-removal programs. "Michigan became the first state in 2013 to demolish homes using money intended to save them," summarizes the *Metro Times* on July 19, 2017. Under the argument that tearing down an unattractive house makes the whole block more attractive—often called the broken windows theory, which is said to simultaneously increase neighborhood pride, reduce crime, and attract new homeowners to an area—more than ten thousand houses were demolished with Hardest Hit Fund dollars, money intended to help individuals facing foreclosure.

The supposed benefit to whole neighborhoods shifts attention away from the gains granted certain individuals. Demolition costs skyrocketed under the blight-removal program, and companies like Homrich—who also performed the majority of the city's water shutoffs—turned impressive profits. "The average price to raze a house had increased 90 percent, from $9,266 to $17,643 by the second quarter of 2016," the *Metro Times* explains. The Detroit Land Bank Authority, the largest holder of land in the city of Detroit and another former owner of my home, is being investigated by a federal grand jury for its role in these demolitions.

———

It's all well and good to be given a free house to write in. For the most part, I enjoy the experience, although I am not sure I would recommend it to just anyone. But when one discovers that the house was acquired by way of several different likely illegal but certainly unethical methods, something about the experience feels so deeply American it sickens. That I am low-income, and miraculously granted access to the American Dream of home ownership, is supposed to keep me from looking too closely at the conditions of my victory. That I am a writer, however, stipulates that I must anyway.

———

I don't want to tell Nandi's story for her. She's a better storyteller than I'll ever be, and you should look directly to her work for whatever of this tale she wants to share. But it's important for you to understand this: she never receives her house.

———

I devise a script and try three phone numbers associated with T—— L—— that I find in various searches through public records. "Hi, my name is Anne Elizabeth Moore and I'm writing a book about a house you might have lived in at [address]. I'd love to ask you a couple questions if you're willing to answer them" is what I intend to say. At the first number there is no answer. The second line is disconnected. At the third, a recorded voice tells me that no one is currently available but that I should try my call again later.

From what I can tell, the first number is associated with one of the addresses tried by the process server in my lawsuit, the one the courts deemed most likely to be T—— L——'s. The second will clearly get me nowhere, but the third holds real promise. It's listed under T—— L—— C——, the previous owner's own full name and another surname, the last name of an associate of

T—— L——'s. The address associated with this phone number was not among those tried by the courts, overlooked by underpaid or busy staffers. I ponder what I might say if I call again.

But later that afternoon: A message. From the third number. A male voice leaves a spontaneous, three-minute rap song on my voicemail. Is it a butt dial? I cannot make out all of the lyrics, but most of them are lewd if catchy. He's not bad. I call back several times to no avail.

I look up the house associated with this phone number on Google Street View. It's extremely cute, with one car parked in the driveway in front of the garage and another on the street in front of the building. It's white, a two-story colonial with a well-manicured front lawn and clever white stone edging around the decorative plants in front, all well cared for. I grow jealous of the occasionally cracked but still passable sidewalks, the massive front yard, the roomy second floor.

To me, it looks like a happy home.

10

HOME

But . . . I had said "but" too often. One cannot go on
saying "but." One must finish the sentence somehow,
I rebuked myself. Shall I finish it, "But—I am bored!"

—VIRGINIA WOOLF, *A Room of One's Own*

Detroit is changing. I come back and: Art-house microtheater! Multiple plant-based restaurants! New wine bar! I visit a city office and file a complaint with the proper municipal authority within an hour! Government documents are available in Bangla!

But most of the landcarpets are gone.

———

"How's Detroit property ownership treating you these days?" ask friends who have followed the legal drama.

"Way too real estate" becomes my standard response.

———

My father takes me to movies very suddenly in the afternoons when he is consumed by anger, although not when it is directed at me. Even at seven or eight I can see that he believes this to be fatherly. Our outings, however, are never announced in advance, so I am otherwise engaged—playing or reading—when they arise. Neither does he check listings, so the film is selected at the box office based on what he will find soothing, with no concern for start times or previous viewings. He often chooses Disney movies. *Lady and the Tramp* I see this way. *Bedknobs and Broomsticks.* My fourth and fifth viewings of *Star Wars*, of many more than that. When the ticket salesperson protests that the movie started an hour ago, he says it's OK, that he doesn't mind. Then we enter the dark theater and the center of the action. Character development, nuanced build of love interests, or unfolding backstories of villains—entire plots are lost to me, and I can only watch events as they unfold on the screen stripped of context.

The first few times, we sit through the film until it ends and then begins again, and when we get to the part where we'd come in, my dad slaps his hands to his knees and says OK. Then we stand up to leave. As I get older, he no longer cares at all how much of the movie we take in. I am around nine or ten when I stop knowing how popular films begin, learn to ask friends to recite entire plots of movies to me, front to back, so I can resolve any lingering plot points. We are at this time arriving in the middle of a film, watching until my father gets bored and strikes his hands to his knees and says OK, and then leaving. One time the film is particularly good and I am delighted to realize he has not been paying attention to it at all. We watch the same film all the way through once and then continue watching it from the middle on, again to the end. He is drunk.

During this period I get very good at immediately assessing the dynamics between characters and, by extension, between people. It's a strange skill, to be able to piece together the beginnings and ends of narratives without benefit of context. Perhaps it's not something I should be grateful my father fostered in me, but I am. Without it I would be lost.

———

The changes in the neighborhood are not necessarily demographic, or rather, they are not changes to the makeup of the people. Mostly, the Banglatown households closest to mine are swelling to accommodate recent immigrants and new babies; perhaps an aging mother or obstinate father has decided to join the family Stateside. Landcarpets give way to safety lights in empty lots and these, in turn, are fenced in. These shifts are subtle, but noticeable, perhaps attributable to slowly rising incomes. They also mirror the city's increased attention to the area. An empty-lot lawn-mowing session will quickly follow a newly poured square of sidewalk, for example. It's important to note that this is not gentrification. But it is change.

———

Setting an asking price for the house takes some consideration. I am told it is worth eighty thousand dollars when it is given to me;

this appears to be an exaggeration of the seventy thousand dollars it cost to renovate, listed on documents now in my possession. The money I put into repairing it, plus two years of appreciation, plus legal fees would allow us to think about pricing the house in the one-hundred-thousand-dollar range, but this is twice as much as any of my neighbors can consider paying for it. I question my own baseline for decisions about pricing, too, for this is when I most feel the pull of my monied upbringing, a sense of entitlement to wealth that is irrelevant to this particular transaction. Then, of course, there are comparable home values. Without a second story, houses in my neighborhood don't generally sell for more than seventy thousand dollars.

Financing options for potential buyers must also be considered. Bank mortgages are becoming more frequent in the city, largely due to a new program from Quicken Loans, although this option is not popular among my neighbors. The Bengalis I know don't rely on banks and won't consider a mortgage. I locate a loan officer who specializes in working with the Bengali community and speaks Bangla; none of the neighbors who inquire about buying my house will agree to speak with him. This makes selling to Bengali folks for more than fifty thousand dollars tricky, unless I want to employ a land contract, which I do not.

In the end, I am left to decide this: Do I price the house at an amount equal to the paychecks I gave up to live in it, plus my expenditures, which would ensure I walk away with some compensation for the endeavor but likely necessitate a white, middle-class buyer? Or do I price the house in a range my neighbors can easily afford and donate the investment that the organization originally made in me to the Detroit community I lived in, even if this makes it unlikely I will ever own another house?

Put another way, this is when I must decide if I will deliberately participate in the gentrification of Banglatown or write off several years of my life as a financial disaster filled with a lot of dark days. This is not an easy decision.

———

During the time the house is off the market to resolve title issues, I receive a series of phone calls. Callers inquire if the house is still available for sale, and I ask how they got my number and why they are calling me instead of the listed real estate agent. "Public records," I am told, and "I am offering cash to you, directly."

"Do not call me again," I say the first few times and hang up. Several speculators do anyway and place offers on my house that are substantially lower than my asking price, hinting at legal troubles or liens they agree not to inquire about.

Soon the number of speculators who call is greater than the number of individuals who came to showings while the house was on the market. None of them increase their offers over time but check in periodically anyway, waiting for my frustration to rise to the point that their bids grow more appealing. I stop answering the phone.

———

Murmurs across porches suggest that my departure might be bad for the neighborhood's image, that the upward shift to the perceived class status of the block may pause in the wake of my absence. I note this from some remove. There is plenty to indicate that my neighbors love me, but linking my presence to upward mobility is about my whiteness, not the strength of my relationships.

———

After three and a half years, including a significant absence and a brief return, as well as two years of nationally recognized reporting on the city, during which writers nationally and internationally refer to me in print as a Detroiter, certain city residents begin to take me seriously as a local. The proprietor of a café recognizes me, calls me an old-timer, and offers me a free coffee. A gallery owner asks if I would like to have a show, an honor only bestowed on locals. An organizer recognizes me at an event and asks about my recent work, poses to me a question that arises about the history of the city. These are kind gestures toward inclusion and I appreciate them, but I am no longer engaged. My coolness regarding this recognition is well received. Acting like you don't care about making it in Detroit earns admirers in Detroit. It reminds me of the social dynamics of an alley behind a donut shop: All the cool kids smoking and scoffing at the world. The easiest way to befriend them is to light up a cigarette a distance away and look bored by their presence. I respect it deeply. It is how I meet most of the people I care about growing up.

———

Woolf's chief complaint about the persistent predominance of what she considers male writers—whom we might now describe as largely straight, white, cisgender, and upper-middle-class male writers—isn't that the monoculture they have unwittingly devised lacks any sense of social justice, racial diversity, or equal rights. It's that the absence of these things has created work that is boring. Repetitive. Unstimulating.

In Detroit I come to a similar malaise. Every new unexplained five-hundred-dollar water bill, every failure to get the streets cleaned, every resident angry about rising property taxes and dwindling job opportunities and lack of support for entrepreneurs. This is all unjust, yes, and deeply wrong. But it is the repetitiveness that I find I cannot abide. The long hours on the phone. The parking and reparking of cars to no end. Weekly trips to city offices, where no one can help unless you go to a different city office. Such tasks add up and place an undue burden on city residents, leaving unpaid locals to do the work that officials are paid to complete. The accumulation of red tape is heartbreaking. But it is also fucking boring.

———

I receive in the mail an unusual postcard. I WANT TO BUY YOUR HOUSE, it says in large, bold letters. The postcard is yellow, the text black. There is a picture. The text printed along the bottom of the postcard addresses me by name: ANNE, I'M AN INVESTOR BUYING PROPERTIES IN HAMTRAMCK, AND I WANT TO BUY YOUR HOUSE. Under this is printed my address, also in bold letters.

In case there remains any confusion about which of my houses the investor is interested in, a black arrow points it out in the picture, which is pulled from Google Street View. CALL NOW FOR YOUR $$ CA$H OFFER $$, the postcard elaborates, promising an as-is sale, no fees or commissions, an immediate response.

The Google Street View image is jarring, an update made in recent months, taken while I was at home, cleaning. All my rugs are laid out on the railing of the front porch, my truck is parked in front of the house and there, a blur at the door: Me. Watched.

Of course, the original house listing did not contain my name; this was pulled from public records, like my phone number. When I receive the postcard, the house is not on the market, still undergoing the quiet title process. So someone has tracked the sale of the house and its removal from the market and has chosen to target me without knowing why the house was withheld from sale. The phone calls offering same I find annoying, opportunistic. But the phone calls never imply I am under surveillance. The postcard, with its emboldened intimacy, feels aggressive, violating. Predatory.

———

I can't believe I've written almost a whole book about Detroit without mentioning how I wanted to be a Supreme when I grew up, without expressing my unending joy at hearing Motown on endless repeat at every grocery store, doctor's office, and street fair I attend.

———

I leave Chicago and plan to return to Detroit for one month to complete the first draft of this book. A week and a half later, my cobbled-together internet, borrowed from a friend, gives out. I can no longer conduct research at home, which means, to a large degree, that I cannot write at home. Or I could put it this way: the free house I was given to write in was not free or mine, nor would it allow me to write. This time I go to New York.

———

A man calls my real estate agent one day asking about house keys. The man, it seems, had seen an ad for my house online, listed as a rental. All of the images from the original sales listing had been taken and posted with the ad, advertising my house, for rent, at a remarkably low price. The man had inquired about the house, expressed sincere interest, and asked about the unusually low rent. He was assured over email that the rental was legitimate but, since the house would move quickly, was urged to submit a security deposit immediately. This the man did. Further emails to his online correspondent went unanswered, however, so the man web searched the address and located my real estate agent, who he assumed had rented him my house. He hadn't.

The police are uninterested in the case, claiming that no crime has been committed and declining to fill out a report. The website that posted the ad is slightly more responsive and pulls the fraudulent listing.

"It happens a lot," the site representative explains.

———

The house is on the market, and then off to resolve title issues, and then on again, a process that takes two years. Finally a young Bengali couple, eager to grow their family, decides to purchase it. However, they require a translator for every interaction, and the couple does not own a computer, so documents must be signed in person, a process that often takes weeks. The first closing date passes with few of the necessary documents completed; the second goes by with even less fanfare. Of course, by now there is a pandemic, historic job losses, and the threat of economic collapse. By the morning of the third closing date, it is unclear what will happen. We have included a provision in the contract that stipulates that the house will go back on the market the next day if the closing does not go through. Then we will start over.

———

My real estate agent grows tired of calling only in frustration and determines to find an upside. "Good news!" he says by way of introducing a new barrier to the sale of the house, conveying a missed deadline, or explaining another skipped closing date. "We've got a whole new chapter for your book!"

———

The house has not yet sold when I finish writing the first draft of this book. I ask and am advised that yes, it would be unprofessional to end a memoir with ellipses, although it does seem like there would have to be literary precedent for this. I try out various endings, but because the sense of relief that I feel at finishing the book does not outweigh my anxiety about still owning the house, I can find no satisfactory conclusion to this text while the story it conveys, of my experience with the house, continues. When I finish this draft it is March 1, 2020. I imply that everything ended happily ever after. And then the world changes.

————

I rent a house for the winter in upstate New York to finish this book, an agreement that is terminated by surprise when the pandemic hits. This is technically an eviction, although my concern for my health as an immunocompromised person takes precedence over my interest in protecting my legal rights. The physical aspect of the move is easy. Most of my belongings are still in storage, so I have little to transport besides books and cats and medicines. Too, I handle the surprise transition and sudden housing search during a public health crisis as genially as possible. Still, the stress of the unexpected move—on top of the anxiety caused by the pandemic as a high-risk person—is enormous. It is no time to write a book about the search for home and housing insecurity. For several weeks, I can barely write my own name.

Detroit Eviction Defense suggests tens of thousands of homes were foreclosed in Wayne County in 2019, most in Detroit, placing thirty thousand families at risk of eviction. This is too many. One is too many.

———

Finally the house sells to the young Bengali couple, so I return to Detroit in September to move out the last of my stuff. Michigan's coronavirus cases are resurging, but I cannot delay the trip any longer. I simply bow my head, mask up, and resolve to survive by any means necessary.

My neighbors are business as usual. Likely they don't interact often with new people and do, in fact, have little chance of contact with infection, but who knows. They employ no masks, utilize no social distancing protocols, institute no changes to the way they pray or prepare food. That I have never been able to sufficiently explain that I am immunocompromised and must take extra health precautions even under normal circumstances now becomes a matter of life or death. I repeat that I must remain masked and distant, that I would love to hug them but cannot. I ask my neighbors what they are doing to protect themselves. "Maybe Bengali people don't get it?" one neighbor suggests, then admits there are active cases a block away.

"But," she clarifies, "not this block."

———

The night before the movers arrive, my neighbors decide to throw me a barbecue. I've never had a surprise party, as in a planned event that I genuinely did not know was going to happen in advance, but the quick execution is a genuine surprise. The whole neighborhood cooks, and then arrives, and I am surrounded by people I have watched grow up over several years and love deeply. However, it is also terrifying from a public health standpoint: a large maskless gathering, plenty of direct contact across multiple generations, food prepared and eaten communally.

And then the youngest school-age girl, one of my favorites, begins coughing uncontrollably.

————

I do not listen to the tape that Melissa and I made over Bengali sweets with the neighbor girls until more than a year after we recorded it, when I am preparing this book. "You should have seen your house before you came, Anne," Sadia says casually as we are preparing to leave the sweetshop. "It was in awful condition. Broken windows. People broke in. There were a lot of stray cats living there."

Nishat, always softer, agrees. "At one point," she says, some people "just came in and lived there. They had parties and everything."

Sadia elaborates. "People would come over to Nishat's house and ask if they could charge their phones, 'cause they didn't have electricity or water or nothing." The two talk over each other now, thrilled by the attention, delighted to be educating me on something so central to my life, my house. I am feeling pressure to ask them everything I can think of while we are together, while the tape is rolling, while their parents have offered permission. None of us know at the time that I will be gone in two months.

As I listen to the recording now, I realize Nishat is describing

T——L——and a friend, maybe her boyfriend. "They were nice," she says. "We used to hang out sometimes. I used to talk to them."

"Were there kids?" I ask on tape, distracted. "Was it a whole family or families?"

Nishat says no. "They had a dog for sure," she adds. "They left the dog in the closet and it was there for a while and we called animal control and they saved it." That part of the story she has told me before, she acknowledges. Then she adds something new, although I miss it in the moment. "A few weeks later the guy came back looking for his dog," she says.

The piece clicks into place. T—— L—— did intend to come back to her house, at least once. The change this makes looks very slight on paper, perhaps imperceptible. But it indicates that the house was seized, not abandoned.

———

I am in New York when Thurber gets sick. In truth Thurber's kidneys have been bad for several years but get worse suddenly. He eats less, cries in pain more often. Has trouble with his sight. One night he sleeps on my chest and is unusually still; in the morning he has trouble with his hind legs. The new kitten, Captain America, has never emboldened herself to offer him any direct affection before but stretches her neck across his back. We all nap together.

I can no longer pretend Thurber is not dying. It has been a process for many months, perhaps years, but now it will be a matter of hours. I wonder if he will simply give up in my arms, but he is not one to give up, not one to leave me willingly. I hold him for the rest of the day, and through the night, and in the morning the vet comes to the house to put him to sleep. She gives him a sedative and I tell him I love him, then she gives him another sedative, more of it, to end his life. Every single moment so painful that there is no worst time, no moment that my grief is deepened or relieved, no change whatsoever.

When the vet takes his body away for cremation, I am alone with the kitten and grieving every harsh word I uttered to Thurber in our twenty-three years together, reliving every ridiculous moment, cherishing every loving comfort, missing the entirety of our relationship. My sorrow grows and swallows up everything else: the moments I did not spend with him, the decisions I made not in his best interest but for myself. My relationship with this cat outlasted my relationship with either of my parents, and this is how I came to define home: where he was to be found.

I cry so hard and for so long that I am no longer crying about these twenty-three years only but about the whole world, about decisions made and unmade, about other cats and other people and the whole past and the entirety of the future. Then I am empty, and ready, and still.

———

Suddenly, a gust of wind, hijabs asunder. Everyone at my going-away barbecue is caught by surprise. So is our dinnerware, disposable, purchased in bulk, and precariously open to the elements on a table on the porch next to great vats of chicken, green salad, macaroni noodles, chips. A giant stack of plates catches the wind and bursts into the air like a flash against the evening's reminder that days and other good things end, an orange and pink sky. The Styrofoam glints, pearlescent, catching for a moment the bright salmon color of the sunset and then flashing pure light, the air suffuse with breathtaking hue. Although we have been speaking of sad subjects—parting—all assembled gasp, young and old, murmuring in English and Bangla. For a moment, no one breathes, eyes wide with amazement. Then everyone laughs, together. It's wonderful: noises of joy illustrated in glittering white and pink, the sounds and tones of comfort and love, filling the atmosphere like fireflies, like aurora borealis.

The plates take to the air for only a moment and then fly away, scattering across three porches to the south, some going farther in the wind. In a moment the phenomenon will become litter, just more rubbish strewn about the forgotten neighborhood of a neglected city, another reason for passersby to roll their eyes, city officials to focus their attention elsewhere. Neighbors who had skipped the barbecue come out to watch the commotion die down and status quo return, ask what happened. "It was beautiful!" Nishat cries, still laughing at the memory. The whole party is cacophonous, boisterous in agreement, before settling into contentment.

By then it is nothing again, just trash on the ground, but Nishat is right, as always.

It is unforgettable.

ACKNOWLEDGMENTS

The following people were instrumental in either the creation of this book or the events described herein, and I remain deeply indebted to them for their support: Liana Aghajanian, the Arreola Martinezes, Toby Barlow, Matilda Bickers, Jenaveve Biernat, Sarah G. Bolling, Laura Bombach, Emmy Bright, Mike Burridge, Nick Butcher, Nick Caverly, Chloe Chapin, Anna Clark, Jace Clayton, Billy Collins, Nandi Comer, Amy Corle, Sarah Cox, Iris Cushing, Kevin Eckert, Ouliana Ermolova, Roz Foster, Rosalie Glauser, Eli Gold, Francis Grunow, dream hampton, A. S. Hamrah, Ashley Hennen, Nicole Hill, Ann Holder, Naomi Huffman, Kimberly James, Alice Jennings, Jennifer Kabat, Sarah Kavage, Laura Ķeniņš, Mike Koftinow, Amanda Kraus, Daniel Kraus, Meiko Krishok, Sheika Lugtu, Jova Lynne, Megha Majumdar, Xander Marro, Moshe Marvit, Joe Mason, Liz Mason, Airea Dee

Matthews, Melissa Mays, Melissa Mendes, Anna Moschovakis, Nadine Nakanishi, Claire Nowak-Boyd, Bridget Francis Quinn, Gina Reichert, Casey Rocheteau, the Salims, Chris Salveter, Tim Schwartz, Matthew Sharpe, Adrian Shirk, Nancy Arms Simon, Zeb Smith, Megan Stockton, the Sultanas, Laura Taylor, Kristina Tuck, Ryan Vandebergh-Malburg, and Robin Williams.

ANNE ELIZABETH MOORE was born in Winner, South Dakota.

In 2019, her book on comics creator Julie Doucet, *Sweet Little Cunt*, won a Will Eisner Comics Industry Award. Her book *Body Horror* was nominated for a 2017 Lambda Literary Award and a Chicago Review of Books Award, was listed as one of 100 Best Books of All Time on the Political Economy by *BookAuthority*, and named a Best Book by the Chicago Public Library. The comics journalism collection *Threadbare* made the 2016 *Tits and Sass* list "Best Investigative Reporting on Sex Work." *Cambodian Grrrl* received a 2012 Lowell Thomas Travel Journalism Award for Best Travel Book. *Unmarketable* was named a Best Book of 2007 by *Mother Jones*.

Moore's essays "Reimagining the National Border Patrol Museum (and Gift Shop)" and "17 Theses on the Edge" received honorable mentions in *The Best American Nonrequired Reading* (in 2008 and 2010, respectively). "Three Days in Detroit," an essay in *The Baffler*, was longlisted for *The Best American Essays 2018*.

Moore is the former editor of award-winning *Punk Planet*, the founding editor of *The Best American Comics*, and the former editor in chief of the *Chicago Reader*. She has exhibited work in the Whitney Biennial in New York; in Leipzig, Phnom Penh, Berlin, Tbilisi, Lisbon, and Vienna; and in a solo exhibition at the Museum of Contemporary Art in Chicago. Moore has been honored with a National Endowment for the Arts Media Arts Award, a UN Press Fellowship, a USC Annenberg/Getty Arts Journalism Fellowship, and two Fulbright Scholarships. She has taught at the School of the Art Institute of Chicago, was a visiting artist at ArtCenter, and was the 2019 Mackey Chair at Beloit College.

She lives in the Catskills with her ineffective feline personal assistant, Captain America.